Contents

Volume 95:2 Summer

Poems

Centrefold

Reviews

Endpapers

POEMS

in the dark we lay hands on the hunger of the sun

—Tomaž Šalamun

Tomaž Šalamun
The Apple

such an Eros? such a home?
it tumbles, reckless, humus of earth
the woods, brilliant steam of night
the smoke, we name the smoke the surface of the sea
who wallows in the vault?
who supports the hunger of the sky?
where will we put earrings, young lieutenants,
weary sailors?
as if the light itself would show us how to pluck an apple
how to smell it, predatory beast
how ink pencils, ice of mirrors
from the hand descend clouds, who seduces fire in the night?
who knows about loam, about weather? who knows how to feed the stove?
herd of hungry mercenary minds
pesky habits, lazy muzzles
Thoth's work coupled common flowerbeds
steam! steam moves souls! textiles!
breaking hiddens slide
monkeys are hungry, runners are hungry
gifts lick straps, the principle trembles
lying down, I will rake fishes, dry colour of crumbs
fencers, baroque stuntmen, huts of mouth
look at loosened world bonds, drunken crickets
buckskin pokes, terrible children
there is bustle in the orbits, rot in mobile fish
break-neck in the height of eagles
wrappers, rivers of angels, raspberries pierced
on earth we do not file flames, we do not foresee God's temples
we do not turn up our palms
on earth we tremble, destroy waters, nourish smoke
in the dark we lay hands on the hunger of the sun

Translated from the Slovenian by Anselm Hollo and the author

One Thousand and One Nights

It smokes from the fridge.
The sun. The sky. The wine.
Pine needles on red earth,
across the bay, the oak.

Deep is the body in the sea,
in the golden mandorla.
The sail splashes the face,
a dunked salty deer.

We're swimming on the other island.
Straight, straight rocks.
The heather is violet, green brown,
the soil is eager.

Translated from the Slovenian by Joshua Beckman and the author

John Burnside
Eleven Gift Songs

Labor to feel the life of God in your soul; labor to make the way of God your own, let it be your inheritance, your treasure, your occupation, your daily calling. Labor to God for your own soul as though there was no other creature on earth. Sweep clean. Ah, sweep clean I say. But, I say, sweep clean.
      —Testimonies of the Life, Character, Revelations and Doctrines of
          Mother Ann Lee, and the Elders with Her

I. Event

Nothing, or everything, matters;
new snow; the light on the asphalt

orange or cherry-red
when the quiet is over;

the car at the end of the street
completing its turn;

a girl walking home from school;
a man with his dog;

how pure occasion
sanctifies the world:

one thing and then the next,
then nothing at all

other than making space
for the life that continues,

the child you have still to name,
the tree in your garden,

this florist's window
lit before the dark:

its perfect golds;
its subtleties of rose.

II. Colour

In my mind's eye, the snow is falling on shingled walls;
a woman is washing a corpse in a lamplit kitchen;
someone has stopped at a gate, to offer the dog
a sweetmeat;
           and, far in the distance,
the blue of a pine is the sum of the visible world;
enough, when it disappears, to begin again:
yellow, then silver; lilac, then tangerine.

III. Time

We had started to feel at home
in these names and skins:

Thursday, the girl from the crescent
walking to school in the dark

with her blinded viola;
Saturday afternoon like a halted bell

and that feeling we had
that nothing would ever happen,

waiting for hours at a time
in the hush of our lives

and watching the weather come in
as if we had planned it:

light in the trees
at the opposite end of the park;

water and falling snow
and a Nazarene sun.

IV. Speech

What do the dying remember,
if not the unspoken?
The intimate fog of scripture, the nightjar's call,
a hint of the yellow to come
in a bowl of persimmons?

As children we had words for how the sun
investigates the surface of a glass,
words for the mesh of a net, or how a shoal
of fishes in their millions, far at sea,
glamoured the sky;

now everything is absent from its name,
florist's shop, asphalt, snow pouring off a tree
and splashing across a pavement, like melting lace:
event, not noun; the transitory
event of the world slipping by, and the world is all.

V. Ashes

Though they say it is only
the white of the brain burning out,

and not the first tentative steps
to afterlife,

I want to be sure, when it comes,
that I see the light

exactly for what it is: no more or less
illusory than any other light,

and surely no more illusion than the dark
where souls go floating, burning out like smuts,

or glimmering a moment, in the heat
between a rice-field and the coming stars.

VI. Gravity

Imagine the world recovered in a touch:
every cobweb of a patient childhood;
fig trees in empty courtyards; mingled cries
and powdered wings along the arteries.
Imagine it: the forms that rise through ash,
the slow curve of a memorised caress
finding the bone and tracing out the lines
of marrow, for that angle in the flesh
where dust remains to name itself again.

VII. Rebirth

It's Kipling who says it, I think,
perhaps in The Light That Failed, where
the hero (whose name I forget)
stares at himself in the mirror and says out loud

'Never go back'.
                    Though maybe it's someone else,
in another book,
coming to quiet grief, or the faint resignation
of one who has seen enough
to accept defeat.
                    Though it's only defeat
while we're calling it something else,
and going back is only the mistake
we count upon, the key that turns the lock

on some far household in the mind itself:
your long-lost raincoat hanging in the hall
and the garden you know from a dream, in an empty mirror,
the holly bush filling with light and the flicker of swallows.

VIII. Anachoresis

You have the right to remain silent;

also the right to choose
the company you keep,

if only the dead, then the dead:

poems and bookplates;
love songs whispered through static.

IX. The life of others

This morning, near the harbourfront, I passed
the undertaker walking to his car,
dressed for the job, but smiling, without that far
off look in his eyes, to show he'd seen the last

of human goodness decked out for the grave
in Sunday best: good wives and honest men,
the likes of whom will never come again.
Or is it just a cigarette he craves

when, standing by the hearse, he tries to seem
not unconcerned, but absent, at the scene
of someone else's grief? He looked so glad

to be so by himself this morning, as the sun
singled him out: alive, in his own dream,
and no one there to counter but the dead.

X. Garden

Death is only a launching into the region of the strange
Untried; it is but the first salutation to the possibilities of the immense
Remote, the Wild, the Unshored.
> —Herman Melville

Summer is ending here, in a drift of smoke:
damp on the walls of the vine-house; mildew and cracks

in the paintwork, where a spider's nest has long since
broken;
  wisps

of gossamer and chitin left behind
like clues to something wider: life itself,

a thousand starlings settled on the roof
and walls; a hapless spill

of pinion-bones and feathers; butcher's broom
and eucalyptus, waiting for the fog.

Out on the meadows someone is tending a fire;
no-one I know, though a shape in his back

is familiar: the care he takes,
the way he holds his rake

familiar, like a sheath-knife or a scythe,
the way it fits the hand, the easy

heft of it.
He does his work the way it should be done,

the way that I would do it, with as little
movement as is needed, with the grace

that comes of being unaware of skill
or effort, and at ease within a world

where nothing else can happen for an hour
but this: the tended flame, the summer's end,

dew on the shaft of the rake
and the light on his hands

turning to gold, then green
as the evening surrounds him.

XI. The afterlife

Sooner or later, you wake in a different season,
the tree you can see from your window, the public gardens,
the bus stop where you disembarked last night
in summer clothes, with music in your head,
buried in snow today, and still, like the cities in snapshots.

How quickly it seems familiar, being dead:
that feeling of a public holiday
in winter; how the time it takes to cross
an empty street, all ridged and scarred with ice,
is suddenly too long; how far away

the others seem, sketched in as afterthoughts
– menfolk in hats and scarves, the hint of a girl –
smudges of water and ash on the morning light,
arriving from nowhere, mistaking themselves for the world.

Paul Batchelor
To Photograph a Snow Crystal

                    Hokkaido, '54.
Ukichiro Nakaya
                    coaxes a crystal
into life on a rabbit hair
                    in an unlikely menagerie
of stellar dendrites
                    double stars
sectored plates
                    crystal twins
clusters, bullets
                    & chandeliers.
The fickle, six-fold
                    symmetry of snowflakes.
The fourteen identified
                    varieties of ice.
Why do complex patterns
                    arise spontaneously
in simple physical
                    systems? Trust me, love,
to make heavy weather
                    of first principles.
What might I make
                    of these arabesques;
facets & lattices,
                    glyphs & ciphers,
the shapes with which
                    you decorate your poems?

Vuyelwa Carlin
Lydia

born 1910

Tiny Lydia, each little bone outlined;
translucent Lydia – the vein-map of you:

your fragile fierce arm clings –
'Help me – I've been wrong all my life.'

Miniature ivory, flake of alabaster,
airy puff of hair; you mark at a touch –

fairyish thing bruised by the pea
twenty mattresses down. 'I'm wrong –

he said so – and you know it –' over and over;
Thumbelina's seed of heart, pinched with cold.

Brittle, pressed blanchflower, you hold on –
the lodged hook drags, and drags.

Ellen

born 1908

'What's your name?' you ask, over and over:
but answers slip off, unlodging.
– Oh, the tiny, stiffening ear-bones quiver still,

grasp at sounds, spin, mould – a word's thrown;
and our names all throng the placeless past –
row upon row, unfired.

Your own name clings about you – 'I'm Ellen.'
Bundle of sticks, a marionette unstrung,
you slump, slide –

you haven't walked in years.
– But pace (as it were) the same little, bleak shore,
strip-walled off with fog, the sea vague beyond.

'A long way to Pen-y-coedcae,
a long way home.' You read (blind)
from the anciently furrowed rocks – sought by poets –

beneath the forest,
its matted deadwood: declaim – softly, almost singsong –
Wanderer, your exile.

Gwyneth Lewis
Happy Flamenco

Don't tell me when to be happy.
I'm losing my mind. No loss,
you say, because outside
oranges ripen in the cold,
to make bitter marmalade. I pray
I'll be put back together in a larger way.

Now that you're with me, back from the dead,
(I didn't turn round! I didn't
turn round!) my heart's
gone missing. It beats like the band
that meets to rehearse by Delícias Bridge
for fiesta or carnival. The bugles are loud
but, for all their practice, they're getting worse.
This is as well as my heart will ever be.

I thought you were gone. But the Guadalquivir
swells each day with a fifty-mile tide
that brought low galleons of New-World gold
to the quays, then didn't. This time round
I'll remember everything and lock it all
in the Toro de Oro of my inner eye.
My body's an empire importing only you.

I saw you drifting on the evening ebb
in a tiny dinghy, no engine, no oars,
under dark eucalyptus. I called
until the herons flew
but you didn't hear me. Don't you know
how strong is the current, how the greedy sea
takes everything to it – dead horses, old shoes,
tree trunks and you, and it won't let go
no, not even when you might have reached
Sanlúcar de Barrameda and the wrecking bar?

Mist covers the river's body like a ghost. Our life
goes through us. You are the bull
I dance with. I no longer know
who leads, who follows but I flick the cloak
as though – *Olé, olé* –
love weren't the ultimate lack of style,
the skill of ensuring that the other survives
in the wet sand, panting to the bullring's roar.
A crimson switch in the back of my eye
and I charge at the lights, at a swordpoint's star.

You say you can't dance, but your blood cells can.
Lymphoma flamenco, full of passionate verve,
technique and *duende*. Deep in the bone
you need a different rhythm now
uno, dos, tres, quatro, cinquo, seis,
no *tarantella*, but the writhe of a snake
tuning the mesh of your DNA,
a *Sevillana*, with viper hands,
stamping on cancer.
Now's the fiesta. *Eso es. Ole.*

Jackie Wills
The Birds Sing About Water

The birds carry a river,
their chorus in my throat,
in the dry spring I walk to,
useless tap, slashed water tank.
I stand in a metal tub with a flannel
waiting for them to fill it drop by drop.

The birds carry a river,
lifted from its source, pulled over
our valley to water mangoes, lychees, tea.
It runs over stones in their beaks.
They shake waterfalls from their wings
drumming pools deeper than feet can reach.

The birds carry a river,
sing until Mashau's roads are rapids.
Fistfuls of pebbles slain on the zozo's
tin roof. Children lay down bottles,
paint buckets, cans. The malachite
kingfisher shows us how to dive.

The birds carry a river
to a priest growling his prayers,
past mercenaries at the plantation gates.
If they could hide it, lay pipes for it,
they would, but the birds carry a river
litre by heavy litre on their heads.

John F. Deane
Tracks

I came rambling out of eternity
scarcely the length of a snipe's flight
from the asphodel meadow; I would go down
into the embrace of clay

testing the haphazard richness
of flag and fern, of cress in the waterlogged hollows,
extravagant dragonflies darting like thoughts
from frond to thorn;

at home you could hear
the turf-sods, in their burning, whispering to themselves
of their own, far-distant past; in the delicious fear
the fire-side yarns offered

I heard the oil-lamp's tongue
tsk tsk against the globe: half-whispered tales
of the devil's hoofprint on the yellow lane, of bodiless
hooded shapes that passed

moaning across the dusk, though soon
this lore would moulder into wisdom, into the Christ's
careful footsteps we would follow through straiter ways.
The meadow waits

not far from the ungovernable sea
where my mind finds rest, imagination comfort; let them say
he is not here, he has gone rambling again by the shore
where the black hag flies, and his Christ.

Threads

Daedalus knew, dull practical artificer,
the shortest distance between islands
is eyes down, and toes tipping the surfaces.
Over the city now snow comes, shawling
everything in winter grey; roofs, windows, spires
disappear with a long sigh into their patienting.
A solitary gull appears out of the gloom, could be
crafted of snow; a balloon, blood-red,
its ribboned plaits dangling, lifts
optimistically, like Icarus, towards adventure.
And out of the gloom comes, too,
perhaps for reasons to do with sorrow, perhaps
the necessary onward
dragging of the day, an image of the old
silent widow, who has licked an end
of black thread, has raised the needle's eye
against failing light and will work on with distressing
patience to stitch something back into place.

Marie-Claire Bancquart

Marie-Claire Bancquart is the author of twenty collections of poetry, as well as critical studies on French literature from 1880 to World War I and essays on contemporary poetry. She lives in Paris, and is a Professor Emeritus at the Sorbonne. This sequence is from Anamorphoses, *co-published in 2003 by Edition Autre Temps in Marseille and Écrit des Forges in Québec.*

from Paris Plainchant

To leave? To see, alone, at home, an insignificant object. To enter. You slip into the city you inhabit, its bread, its mica. Major transgression.

*

Woman,

in a subway car's window, in a tunnel

you glimpse your face
not very clear

resembling
a distorted photo, which you wouldn't keep.

*

The passenger facing you is recounting the history of her house, built in nineteen-hundred by her great-grandfather,

interrupts herself, asks:
"Do you know if the nails of the dead keep on growing for a long time?
I dreamed that his son's, my grandfather's,
had come through the wood of the coffin."

You look at each other with discomfort.

You have tampered with
something not of this world.

*

Unknown lands
so white
long ago
on maps.

What is impossible:
  to flow
  invisible into
      their cliffs.

One reconciles oneself to mapping life
marking small things within its disorder

grass growing between paving-stones

a strange woman's smile in the subway

an advertisement for sardines
which send us back to the high seas, to our fish ancestors

to the hurricane.

Against nothingness
we claim possession of our nothings, our solemn signs.

*

Our highways at crossroads.

Triangular generalizations
surrounded with cement, populated by grass
as wild

as scraps of paper, rags brought by the wind.

Nobody's property
which we see from our cars
more isolated than railroad tracks
which can be followed on foot.

An exile's dream: to become
owner, at least, of this reverted property
only approachable through
the moon's mouth
or a bird's fluttering.

To be able to say: I am the sole proprietor
of that which no one would think to sell
and which provides
all the same
an imagined sweetness.

*

It's the season of rain, of magazines
with wrinkled covers
that one buys on the run
to read on the bus to the Gare St-Lazare.

Impossible to open them
the wet coats are crowded together.

Your attention is seized by your neighbour's mouth
she must have broken up with
someone close   life perhaps
she has tried
has put lipstick
on her fissure-lips

you don't dare look at her eyes.

In the wet woollen odour
you get off;
in the bus-shelter, you read the title on the cover:
We have lost music.

Good morning Rimbaud
it's true
"Academic music does not satisfy our desires."

*

The rain rains down, the faithful spring rain.

You'd think you were in the country. Through a gap in the raindrops, you see a man asleep, his window open, on a bed with carved wood panelling. He has placed (why) a hammer on the ground, near him. You'd like to stay there, in that clearing in the Place des Invalides, and know what he'll do when he wakes up.

In the village, the house in the North had a familiar odour: black soap and coffee. People kept their distance. The most affectionate expression grandmother addressed you with was "my girl."

On her start-of-the-century bodice (the last one, the twentieth) embroidered dots brushed the areolas of her breasts with their shadows.

Used again as a hat's veil on a mouth of the nineteen-forties, they drank in a fog of breath.

Now, between our fingers, on a scarf, they swell with memory.

This scene in a haze of steam
memory crossed by the wind:
little exoduses
disturbed by
the tiny sound of rain on asphalt.
You move away.

The sleeper hasn't even turned over, his face always towards the vast square, for once deserted. The vast beach.

Translated by Marilyn Hacker

Sean O'Brien
A Little Place They Know

To say that the sessions are long is to call
The Crusades 'an affray'. To say that you don't
Understand what the hell's going on
Is like finding Babel 'a little confusing'.
Here in the old world the clocks can run
Backwards or sideways at random, and when,
On the brink of despair, your turn is called –
By then you hardly recognize your name.

How suddenly empty the chamber becomes,
How discreet the Mercedes that spirit
Their regretful delegations homeward.
Now the clocks look at you pointedly. Quick!
You read to seven dead Bulgarians
And then they read to you, and afterwards
They take you to a little place they know
In a hole in the wall of the graveyard.

You wake now. The plates have been cleared. Your hosts,
Obedient to curfew, have departed.
The moon waits, and down at the end of the street
In its washed-out blue engineer's jacket
The sea too is tidelessly waiting, so
All you can hear where the waves ought to break
Is the fizz of butt-ends in the water
Drowning faint renditions of 'Volare'.

Yes, you tell yourself, *let's go – Thalassa,*
Thalassa, you know my true name – the stars
Awake when you and I take ship. But this
Is the shore that comes back through the mist
And the name of your death for this evening
Is Constantin Harbour, 1916,
Museum and slaughterhouse, beautiful hole
In the wall of the graveyard. Do step aboard.

A Coffin-Boat

In Memory of Barry MacSweeney

Today you must go for a walk in the dark. Go in
Where the stream by the graveyard falls
Into the tunnel and hurries off hoarse with graffiti.
You will be hauling a brass-handled narrowboat,
Mounted with twin candelabra, containing
A poet who managed to drink himself dead,
With heroic commitment, a year short of fifty.
Packed up with books and manuscripts and scotch,
In his box from the Co-op, a birthright of sorts.

Get used to the visible stink. It will cling
In a tissue of soot to your hair. Get used
To the silence that stares and says nothing,
A graveyard of clocks with the time on the tips
Of their verdigris'd tongues. You should neither
Look back nor examine your luminous gaze
In the water. This place (the word is used loosely)
Gives off an air of religion decayed
To aesthetics and worse. At least one of everything
Finds its way here to this copyright Hell.
Item, jar of cloudy eyes; item, carved
From bone, a grove of hatstands; item,
Detachment of ambient gargoyles with knouts;
Miscellaneous slick coils of excrement
And rag. And down the dripping galleries
Cartoons of howling inmates hang for sale
Between the stacks of disused literature,
Including some of his – and curiosity
May set him knocking on the lid for one more
Read, but don't you stop: down here's the speechless
History of everything and nothing,
Poetry's contagious opposite. Go on
To the imaginary light.

                    Much later, far up,
Cries of gulls; a weedy birdlimed gate
That opens on the Ouseburn's curdled trench. Go on.
A mile upstream the tide turns back
Round weedy knobs of brick and stone
And clags of grot that wind themselves on mooring-rings.
Here is the rubbled anonymous slipway, left
Among black warehouses designed to look
Resigned and stoic in the hands of lawyers.
They are waiting out the era of unwork
When all the clocks run sideways
And the workers are walking the roads daylong
(From famine road to Scotswood's but a step)
Or imbibing the milk of amnesia. This place
Will be nothing, was nothing, is never, its tenses
Sold off one by one until at last the present stands
Alone like a hole in the air. But still
This is history, this silence and disuse,
This non-afternoon, and it must also serve
Biography – to whit, your man's, for here he goes
Out through the space left for comments made
Over the coffin. You and I, my friend,
And all the rest who have found their way here
Down Jesmond Dene and under Byker Bridge –
We must give an account of our presence.
We shall have to find words for the matter. So, then:
We've come on account of inadequate answers
To phone calls at midnight, to phone calls
Ignored and left ringing. We've witnessed
Italianate umbrage in bar-rooms, read
The poems of recovery and relapse and wondered
What in God's name could be done, and as we did so
Heard the rumour and the death confirmed.
We remember his anger and hurt – and our pity,
That futile and dutiful feeling that hasn't a map
But relies on itself to continue, that shrivelled
When met with the fact of his rage like a bucket of lava

Flung over the listener. Rage. It was tireless
And homeless, and though it walked out on the body
It could not be quenched by affection
Or drink: even now, at the death and beyond, oh yes
It must carry on dragging its grievances into the dark,
For the want of a nail, of a home, of a matchbox,
A drum of pink paraffin, anything fiery enough
To let the man rest by the waters of Tyne.

In *Underworld,* Poetry Review 95:3 —

publication date October 17th 2005

Sasha Dugdale and Ruth Fainlight *In Conversation* ☙
the Long Poem: John Fuller, Tim Liardet and John Burnside
☙ Sean O'Brien on reading Rilke today ☙ poetry from
China, Mexico and New Zealand ☙ Colette Bryce,
John Kinsella, Sarah Maguire, Robert Minhinnick,
Peter Porter & more ☙ *Letter from Dublin* ☙
reviews of Hirshfeld, Lian, Oswald, Morrissey, Petit,
Stevenson, Strand, Sweeney...

Tim Liardet
Loy's Return

To be on your back, says Loy, mashed, while the stuccoed
saloon bar lurches up and dreams it floats
or dips into the wave, and the room goes bending and rolling;

to be nose-up in one boot, while the barmaid calls to you
for some unknown reason in French, *fucking* French.
Nu, this; *Vu* that. *Bonwee* or *Bonwat,* or something

like that. To claw your way up from the floor of the gents
by the taps, says Loy, setting off the hand-drier
to which you mouth a greeting, then drop back,

and having learned how tricky swimming is
after seven years and three months, a week,
a day, three hours inside, he says, to wake to find yourself

staring up from under water and holding your breath
until there's not a bubble to tell anyone you're there,
not a *fucking* bubble, if you'll pardon the French.

Immanuel Mifsud

Immanuel Mifsud was born in 1967. He is the leading Maltese writer of his generation. He has written for the theatre and published several books of stories, as well as two collections of poems, Fid-Dar ta' Clara *(At Clara's House) and* Il-Ktieb tar-Rih u l-Fjuri *(The Book of Wind and Flowers).* Confidential Reports, *a selection translated by Maurice Riordan, is published by Southward Editions/Cork European Capital of Culture.*

I'd Dreamt This Dream Already

Look: even my solitude has died.
Every time I walk I see many walking
behind, in front, beside me... walking
with their hands, their eyes, locked in mine; walking
near me, at rest or upright. Always walking.
They even drink the tears I weep.
Stride after stride, while my face disintegrates
and they pick its remains from the ground.
Stride after stride, while I clear the way ahead.
Stride after stride, and they are always walking:
behind, in front, beside me; walking
near me, resting or upright. Always walking.
I can feel the warmth from their looks.
I even feel the rain that washes them.
I even feel their legs strain to give birth
to more faces to look at me, looking.

Stride after stride, I've dreamt this dream already
when emerging old from the vagina
to find innumerable hands of welcome.
That day also, I'd already dreamt this dream.

Translated by Maurice Riordan

Ruth Fainlight
Almost Immortality

       Almost immortality: to be
remembered for centuries
       like Azade, slave-girl
of Bahram Gur in Firduz' s *Shah Nama* tales

mounted behind, arms tight around his waist
as they hunt gazelles
       on a gilt and silver plate

which survived fire and earthquake
       warfare and plunder
through the long Sassanid dynasties;
to be admired today by you and me.

Robert Saxton
Glow-worms

All splatter, splurge and splinter flower abroad,
    the ride to earth on homemade wiring's hooves.

Fireworks are more than glow-worms can afford,
    living together, though under different roofs.

Pascale Petit
The Hudson Remembers

From Riverside Drive, I stared at you
until I was in a trance.
And the trance-river was long, wide,
and glistened like a great tower
which reared into the sky.
I saw your waves were panes of glass
polished by the autumn rays.
I saw, along your length,
your windows unzipping –
splinters of plate glass stung my cheeks.
You were so bright and wrong,
as if our sun had plunged from his office
and was laid on a stretcher.
I heard a thundering in your bed
that was our star's throes.
Then I realised that your flowing
to the ocean was a falling
that would never end.
People inside you, on a hundred floors,
in your rooms, at your desks.
In your stairwells, your lifts,
in your corridors, swept by currents.
And they were breathing smoke
as if drowning in black water,
charred by flames of river-cold.
And your twin – East River –
also remembers, as it falls with you
into the Atlantic. Where seabirds
dive into debris like airliners.
And the continental shelf drops away.
There, reams of scattered papers
float down into the abyss,
until all their addresses are erased.

Pauline Stainer
The Convoy

Not the profound machinery
of gods,
but military vehicles
coming from great distance,
headlights scenting
the sandstorm.

A more intense country –
the light dropping its guard
on the great dust
of the world,
sand-vipers
in their hot yellows

and beyond,
as if there were no
rules of engagement,
racks of new-dyed sarees
billowing
the scarlet wind.

Ghost Writers to the Emperor

They still inhabit language,
caught between the unsaid
and the unsayable,
hands dappled as apricots
in the latticed light

making their mark
like elephants at a salt-lick,
until only the text
and its inspired omissions
risk the silence.

Mantegna's Hares

We looked out –
the weather whistle-blue,
hares running with the wind
above water
where the sun never reaches.

Give me
the pulse of a hare,
that zigzag between
breath and the moment –
Mantegna's hares, still boxing
beside the agony in the garden.

Tara Bergin
Dancing

All the branches of the plum tree
are in flower and you are dancing
in your sleep.
Serbia is in your hair.
It is a white flower.
It is your right foot.

Serbia's arm is young
around your waist.

All the flowers are gone.
The plum tree's branches
are bent with weight.

C. K. Williams
Plums

1.

All the beautiful poems
about plum trees in flower,
gold in the moonlight,
silver in the silvery starlight,

and not one of them mentions
that the damned things
if you don't pay attention
will pull themselves apart.

2.

A perfect wall of the hard
green globules of pubescent
plums we found
too late deep in the foliage of ours;

both largest limbs
already fatally fractured
had to be amputated,
the incisions sealed with tar.

3.

None of the poems mentions
either that when the hiding
fruit falls, the same flies
that invade to inhabit

fresh dog-shit are all at once
there in the muck of the plums
already rotting their flesh
off as fast as they can.

4.

Abuzz, ablaze, they crouch,
the flies, in the ooze,
like bronze lions it looks like,
drooling at the chance

it looks like to sink up
to their eyes in the rankness,
to process it for their next
thousand generations.

5.

While our once-lovely tree
waits naked in the naked
day-glare for branches
to bring leaves forth again,

and fruit forth, not for us,
nor the flies, but just to be
gold again in the moonlight,
silver in the silvery starlight.

Conversation:
Odia Ofeimun and Ismail Bala Garba

Two of the best Nigerian poets, the senior national figure and a new young writer from Kano – both sometime residents of Oxford – meet in the pages of PR.

*O*dia Ofeimun's political activism and role as poet are inseparable. Formerly Private Secretary to the late Chief Obafemi Awolowo, and Editorial Board member for the* Lagos Guardian, *he has also been President of the Association of Nigerian Authors. Under the military dictatorship he was Chair of the radical collective of* The News. *Ofeimun's major poetry collections are the controversial* The Poet Lied *(1980), which addresses the Biafran war;* A Handle for the Flutist and Other Poems *(1986); and* Under African Skies *(1990).*

After the Coup

for Chinweizu

There are those who have no grace to fall from

buried already in landslides moonslides
and seaslides of collective pronouns:
'we the people',
       we fertilize the day
for sowers whose hands brim with maize
from the silo of tomorrow's famine

we are those who have no grace to fall from
trapped by time and overrun by rented mobs
'we the people',
       carried famously
through gunsmoke by dawn broadcasts
we hallow public squares to welcome
Generals who bend stalk away

from the seeding rains of July,
the silo of tomorrow's harvest,
the stock of fate in answered prayers

we are those who have no grace to fall from
blitzed by hurrahs for the roads never built
for old streets renamed where to rename
is to open history to stock and barrel
which shall be renamed again to humour us
'we the people', journeying without maps

we journey towards maps
bled by Generals in tanks
in a hero-hood of the forgotten

ii

ah! beloved Generals dreaming of manifestos
you who turn cornrows into a field of flags
green and white flags hoisted with gunsmoke

you turn the field into abattoirs of words,
big, grating words planted in tantrums
of iron hooves growing more than wheat or yams

beloved generals more eloquent than manifestos
you are the sheep lionized by suppliant grass
where your mind-cuffs guard our houses of hunger

before every cockcrow and before anvils speak,
ripping the loincloth of dreams from inspired flesh,
your mind-cuffs braid a dance ahead of the muezzin

– sentinels of the dark whose footsteps are slogans
– sentinels of the dark whose acres forbid whistles
– sentinels of the dark whose birds do not fly

your mornings speak of masquerades returning
ancestors returning as abikus seduced by medallions
your mornings seethe with banners and brave fables

dripping with fat to nail stomachs to dank walls
your mornings rehearse amnesia in fiestas and blazes
where our dreams brave gun smoke to fertilize time

Teargas and Gun Smoke

I walk among my people
in teargas and gun smoke
among the passionate
who have lost love;
among the wise
who levitate above answers
in sand dunes that sift
the biography of pain
from the sahel to the lagoon,
the Delta to the Lake

I walk among my people
who do not want to choke
in teargas and gun smoke;
where tyres burn
a necklace of defiance
around every street corner
and fervour runs deep,
in the tindered silence
of breasts uncovered
to nurse lips for swearing

I walk among my people
whom I no longer recognize
as the sun's face is covered
with the smudge of a boot
and the laughter heard
on the streets at night
is the vowel of iron heels
digging dark craters
for those who have nothing,
'Nothing to declare',

I walk among the living,
eyes peppered by dust haze,
broken vows wreaking
wishfulness and nightmares,
tawdry hamattans
steeled by an empire of bats
noising contentment
for knee-buckled causes
and reformers yellowing
in a green wind of decrees

I walk among my people
whose dreams walk with me
where wishes run aground
in bazaars and graffiti
in dark powers of incense
that normalize fear as fate
I walk among my people
knowing that those who live
by bayonets and teargas
must choke in blunderbuss

I walk among the thirsty,
toasting the fisher of fate
in every tributary,
waterfall and confluence
I walk among the slakers, too
affirming the purest water
in hopes that wined the Niger
before the Delta pulsed
through arteries of black gold
to get the sea drunk

Creativity

Simply being ourselves is the complicated shore
to which our voyaging returns

after we have become so multiple
the labour of hearts measured in geographies...

the selves rounding out the risen sun
enter the spheres in tongues of fire.

Lonely amidst crowds, harried by contentions
the body seeks the light that is mine but also yours

owned by the tree, the egret, the wind,
the groaning mountains and the clouds

the light in whose rays God becomes us.

We who can no longer be offended by curses
or replenished by praise

in fullness that remains pure vesselling
beyond work-a-day abuse, above time that debases,

we grow into our own emanation of incandescence
imperfect containers of the perfect flare,

we flow and will not be blocked or else
floods, whirlwinds and typhoons
overtake the simple and the ordinary.

Seeking balance to troubled ecology
we defeat death by living
beyond the claims of matter.

Ismail Bala Garba teaches English at the Department of English and French, Bayero University, in Kano, Nigeria. He has published academic articles and poems in many anthologies, journals and newspapers both in Nigeria and abroad, including New Writing 13.

Where We Come From

Old habits live long, as in the class
we pass the pen between us like a stamp
of despair. One of you today.
The demeanours are different, little passions
bursting up across the desk. They have put
a book on the side over which
we tactfully ignore our memory.

How do you dream? Something fishy
like Our Vow flips out. I know
you are still too thrifty to pay the debt.
Our new hearts wait behind us surprisingly,
with the silent shocks. I think
of all the easiness of gain but, yes,
I'm satisfied now. Yes. Satisfied. Now.

Dear, whatever it was that filled
such bound pages with word
has long been done. It is a book,
measures history. Perhaps the cover.
I see our ethics continuously eroded as
you switch to yours the manner you used
to switch to me. I switch to mine. And

Skill

This is the phrase *mountain climbing*. Now picture
a person, trudging in the place
between our imaginations. He catches our attention.

There is no phrase *safety first*.

You imagine him fail, don't you?
I supposed as much; he suffers but triumphs.
The phrase *loud ovation* is scribbled all over him.

After and Before

I want to reach there late when the mopping
has since been done and you can't smell detergent.
Or when, in the restaurant, tomato and onion
walk all the way down the salad and the garnishing's
just right. Or after the shop closes, when mountains
of mangoes and pineapples still exhibit signs of ageing.
When the lawn's been formally raked, the roses raided
and everything said that could be misinterpreted.

Or before. When traces of tyres and flattened cans
show where the campfire has been lit.
When the beds are made and the guests ushered.
When the repair van drives in and the house
seems like a crime-scene. When there is all the traffic.
When everything has gone right that is going to go right,
all the fixings have been done and grasses begin
to find their ways through the garden.

ℬ

Ziba Karbassi
Blood-home Dance

When the blood-home is here, just here
When the blood-home has the smell of your body
Don't pull me away from myself
                don't take me anywhere away from myself
When the smell of my love's body spreads through the air of the room
                  and the room becomes drunk
And I and the memories and the shadows walk drunkenly
                    with each other
                      and die a little
                        in each other

Dance crazily, dance, blood home dance,
                blood   home   dance

Migrant memories will come back again
Piece by piece memory of the craziness of being apart comes back again
And the cold and the homelessness come to this room
                under this roof
                    to take me away again.

Memories of my grandfather, uncles and aunts
I and my father doing the round loop of Shahgoli
                  and Golistan

The tears of my always grieving mother in the afternoons of summer
  That soft thyroid full of constricted sobbing & fingered by winter bones
Hey, Hey, Hey: all these
              vagrant memories!

Don't take me from myself
            don't take me anywhere at all out of myself

When the smell of jasmine and pomegranate and grandmother, of vanilla
and quince and auntie and saffron, and tangerines and uncle and thin flakes
of nougat, thin flakes, come: it is the hug of my poem, baklava garden,
Tabriz-heart, Shams-breath,
poem-embrace

When grandmother is dead, and auntie too, and uncle
is dead,
and pieces of you are also dead inside me,
why do your chest and my breath still
smell with life?

Don't let them take away my breathing
don't let them cut down my breath-line

And the hair on your chest which is soft
and my head that always falls there

My always peaceful homeland, my always May-time meadow
Let me stay here
just here

Blood-land embrace, poetry-embrace, mother-embrace,
poetry-heart, dear love:
don't let me be pulled away from myself
don't let me be pulled loose
from here at all.

Translated by Stephen Watts and Ziba Karbassi

Shahgoli and Golistan are the names of parks in the poet's birth-city of Tabriz.

Matthew Sweeney
The Sweatmark

The sweatmark on his teeshirt that day
made a map of Ireland, not the map
you'd see in a current atlas, but one
like the ur-map that hung on his wall
at home – where it never got this hot,
not in a hundred years. He wiped
his leaking brow with his half-sleeve
and held the base of the teeshirt out
to look at the sweatmark again.
It was Ireland, all right, even seen
upside down. His own county,
Donegal, was over his right nipple.
Kerry kicked towards the liver
while Dublin was nowhere at all.
He sleeked down his warm hair
with his fingers. What did this mean,
if anything? He got sweatmarks
all these days, but never a map before.
Was it a signal calling him back?
Why else was the teeshirt only marked
in that spot, unlike every other time?
He wondered should he phone home.
Then that voice in his head he hated
told him to take the teeshirt off
and shove it in the laundry basket.
If it really was a map and a sign
it would survive the launderette –
which it didn't, not that that proved
anything, he afterwards thought.
But that sweatmark never reappeared.

Tobias Hill
The Nightworkers

Long after midnight
the railwaymen
work in pairs along the line
surreptitiously, at first,

the track stones
under their boots
trod like ice
into ruts.

The clocks stop for them.
Nothing comes
while they mend their ways.
Nothing goes. The night trains

rest in their stables.
The mainline lies
bright as cobweb

and the voice of the first man to speak
becomes a grand thing in the darkness
and the workers who follow
lope like so many bogeymen
through the lights of the gantry towers.

*

We lie awake for hours.
We rise like sleepers
hauled from beds of stone.
We cannot close our ears to the North
the railwaymen bring in their laughter.

Only towards morning will a word
turn them, one by one
homewards, calling names
and names and goodbyes as they go,

and though we'll be released by sleep
we'll lie awake in those small hours
until we're sure we've heard the last
there is to hear. We'll hang on their words,

listening for the lightness in them,
the lift in their voices at first light,
the eagerness they have in going home,
and even for the way they seem
to wake from sleep or dreams themselves,

as if they've slept their lives away, and now
find themselves boys again, waking in winter
to yell their names clear across miles of snow.

John Stammers
Ten

after Catullus
for EB

I was on my way to an afternoon's loafing
in *Cicero's* coffee house in Drury Lane
when out pops my mate Ed who knows just everyone
(literary family, connections up the ying-yang).
'You must meet Camellia, she's in the next Jude Law'.
A wannabe all the way up, I think, but built! –
micro-skirt, tits like volleyballs –
a solid 10, I say to myself.
'Delighted', I drool.
'How was the States?' asks Ed.
'It's all gone down the original plug,
the war and the paranoia epidemic –
Osama under every trashcan.
Wendy's bought an estate near Oxford.'
'She the one who gave you her Aston Martin?' he asks.
The minx's eyes ignite,
'Oh Johnny', (*Johnny!*) she purrs,
'Could you bear to give me a lift up to Elstree?'
She shifts the weight of her sweet little backside;
her thighs kiss like delicate lesbians.
'Well, naturally, what I meant is
she gave me the *use* of it, *sometimes*.
I spoke using what's called a *convention*,
as you'd've realised if you had half a brain
you talentless little bimbo.'

Daljit Nagra
Father to Father

Grasping – in a suit, at the garden door – my hand,
father has returned from India, skips past me with
a briefcase.

His turban is a bloated bead of ladoo light,
his face – a massive sunflower with its head a honeycomb –
murky,

pocked over me. He's grown by inches. The pulp
of his open mouth aubergine, as he gulps through the room like
an eel

stretching past an *El Greco* which has replaced his Golden
Temple, flashed over my coral of white goods,
shaking

as though to dry himself, now beached in the lounge,
no grain of proof, in our years apart, of a sari
bride.

Crouched by my fireplace, he wizens. Blowing up bubble gums
of air through his balled mouth, he expands like a soufflé.
Puffs

on the flesh of his wagging case till it splits its plum-guts:
its jam of honking parables, prayers, hymns, ex-
orcisms:

each bird's its song that soars, then surveying, shrieks
for its nest, then pikes into window branches to pecker the
glazing.

My father slumps, tears on his arrowy beard are
molasses, his teeth lily leaves on the lower lip,
sharked

at the arrival, by the space hopper, of my son, my wife –
freckled. His briefcase bleeding into sleep by him . . .
O father!

Ladoo – saffron coloured sweetmeat

Marzanna Bogumiła Kielar

* * *

how close you are, blackthorn twig: smooth
as the skin of young apple trees
the silence inside me: not even a bird sings

only fire

Translated from the Polish by Elżbieta Wójcik-Leese

Stephen Watts
I Drove the Sheep Down from the Mountains

I drove sheep down from the
mountains, Nonno. I drove sheep
down off the rock crests and off the
sharp slopes. I drove them without
dogs. In small numbers as they were,
five or six at a time. I was able to do
that. I had that ability. That
confidence. I was nineteen, twenty.
Ages you were when you were still
shepherding in the Alps. I would go
out and find a few strayed sheep and
gather them together and drive
them down to the fank or to the
pens behind the hut. It was on the
islands. Out beyond Skye. Out in the
sea. The east side of North Uist.
Schists and gneisses that were near
on four thousand million years
there. Astonishing remnants.
Geologies that I felt in my body.
Black pseudotachylites that flowed
down off ridges. I've not been back
in twenty-five years. What does that
matter: people were driven from
those shores a century and a half
ago. Cleared. More. Years even
before you were born. Put away for
sheep to St. John's or Newfoundland
or Tasmania. Much the same as you
though: leaving the land and
migrating. Sometimes across a small

island from one side to the other. Sometimes across a sea. Sometimes from the stretto of high valleys to the depths of huge cities. From the nomadic lie of an intuition or the tensions of an economy irrevocably breaking down. I drove sheep down off the mountains, Nonno. Like you, though I did not realise that until years later. I went and found sheep that had stayed out all winter behind the mountain or that had ventured in summer to all the points of the peninsula. One time I went as far as Bagh Morag and sensed seven sheep on a far neck of land and drove them back close to the shore four hours until we were back at the home pasture. Another time we went out to the ram's island at the edge of the sea and I jumped down beside the ram from a rock and held his horns to secure him at the same moment. A big drift-boat that to cart plenty of sheep. That was a far rim of Europe, Nonno. That was a sharp place to fall from the edge of. I wish I'd kept a journal of those days: I'd read it to you now. I would remember with a proper blessing all the grace notes in your life. Otters rose in sea pools to watch for movement on the shore. Owls flew near my face on the moor crests at dusk. A sudden cleft in the treeless island had a rowan bush and a floor of gull-sewn bluebells. Bog cottons

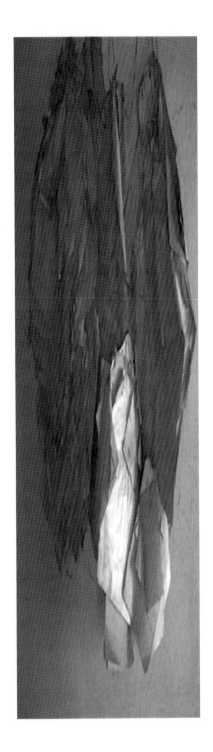

and myrtle that transformed the
meadows and moors. I stayed there
three years, my university. But it was
harsh what was done to language.
Harsh what the mother tongue had
been put through. Harsh what
winters of imperialism did. Nonno,
wasn't that a nomadic century in a
time of comfort. If I were to walk
from North Uist to the Alta
Valcamonica, from the eastern shore
of a western island to the last high
village in a European snowstorm,
what languages wouldn't I learn on
the way. And if I went via
Drohobycz. And if I went through
Olomouc. And if I went by Yerevan.
And if I went with Rumi of Tabriz.
And if I went with my son. And if I
carried my daughter. And if I went
without guns. And if I went via
Nellore. And if I went by Chennai.
And if I stayed places along the way.
What languages wouldn't I learn on
this journey. What words wouldn't I
arrive with at the place of negative
theologies. We drove sheep down off
the mountains and a century passed
by in the blink of our eye.

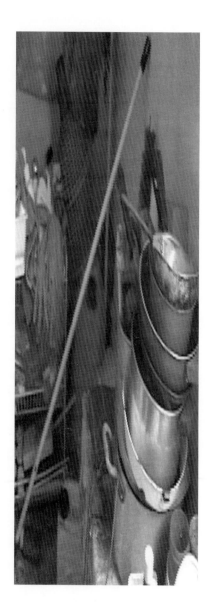

Images courtesy of Amanda Ravetz, from the video installation "Clearings",
a collaboration between Stephen Watts and Amanda Ravetz.

CENTREFOLD

Travelling into the Quotidian:

Some notes on Allison Funk's 'Heartland' poems

JOHN BURNSIDE

In this memory, it's a warm, late October afternoon in East Kansas. I'm maybe twenty or thirty miles west of Emporia, near the Cottonwood River, when I come across a little road that looks like it might need investigating, a road I just know, at a glance, will peter out somewhere in gravel and dirt next to an old wooden farm shack and a dead tractor, or at the edge of a yard where a fat, gun-shy dog sits dreaming on a broken porch, next to a plot of jimsonweed and pumpkins. This is Osage country, the gnarled, bitter fruits of the Osage orange scattered along the banks of the rivers and gullies like live green rubble in the one section of Kansas that isn't pancake flat, right at the edge of the Flint Hills; and even if the old prairie is gone, a few oases of bluegrass remain, not blue now, but rust-red and coppery and golden in the autumn light, last tatters of the real Midwest preserved by government decree to remind the casual visitor – me, for example – of what made this land so magical in our great-great-grandfathers' time.

So I make a detour – a detour within a detour, really – and turn off the highway, knowing I will see nobody for miles, and glad of the fact, wanting to imagine myself alone in the world for a while, travelling in *splendid isolation*, that singular luxury that a place like the Midwest still sometimes affords. There is nothing remarkable about this road and it leads to what is usually called nowhere – which is why the rest of my day is so pleasant. I don't want local colour; I don't want the picturesque; I do not, under any circumstances, want anything recognisable as history. I want the here and now, the divine quotidian, the subtler beauty of the unremarkable. As I drive, I see no real landmarks, other than the occasional cottonwood, nestled into a gully, turning water into shade, and the odd stretch of fence – wood, not wire – around what looks like a derelict farm, but may well be somebody's entire life. To a casual visitor, this is one of those magical places where nothing happens; which is why, when I return a few days later, I cannot find it: no cottonwoods, no dark farms, not even the turning where I first entered this hinterland. I drive for miles and I watch for it all the way, but I never see it. It was an illusion, a phantom, the Kansas version of *Brigadoon*. Later still, when I get back to my borrowed porch and study the map, I can't find anything that corresponds with the road I had driven, on that now already mythical afternoon. Mythical – yes, for me, at least, it was, and is: a chapter in the narrative of real-self that has no particular significance (or not, that is, when it is recounted at second-hand); not even a chapter, really, but a fleeting idea, an image, a metaphor.

"*Il y a un autre monde, mais il est dans celui-là*," says Paul Eluard. To speak of another world has, historically, been to commit to an essentially mystical or religious agenda, and so to a province of wishful thinking normally inhabited by children and the simple-minded, as opposed to the real, factual, *less deceived* world of grown-ups and rationalists. A good deal of argument has gone into the (re)definition of terms like 'mystical', 'religious' and 'rational', but Eluard's remark points us in another direction altogether: the other world is *here, now,* but we pass it every day, we miss it, we see what we expect to see and we think of it as we (are) expect(ed) to think. Eluard's entirely secular programme was to uncover that *autremonde* – that non-factual truth of being: the missed world and, by extension, the *missed self* who sees and imagines and is fully alive outside the bounds of socially-engineered expectations – not by some rational process (or not as the term is usually understood) but by a kind of radical illumination, a re-attunement to the continuum of objects and weather and other lives that we inhabit. We might say, if we could strip away the accretions of dogma and prejudice that have attached to the gospels over centuries, that Jesus's argument – the Kingdom of Heaven is *at hand* – differs very little from Eluard's, and that he too was demanding of his listeners the spiritual and political discipline to bring forth their true selves, in order to see the world in its fullness (or, as *The Gospel of Thomas* puts it, "His followers said to him, 'When will the Kingdom come?' 'It will not come by watching for it,' he said. 'It will not be said, *Look, here it is,* or, *Look, there it is.* Rather the Father's Kingdom is spread out upon the earth and people do not see it'"). Yet it makes as much sense to call this a philosophical or political enterprise as to label it 'religious', for this discipline of the imagination is the central human concern and, without it, there can be no compassion, no good judgement, no justice. Without it, we are lost, in a world we do not know but try vainly to control, according to a set of self-imposed limitations and inherited fears; without it, we are exactly where the powers-that-be want us: malleable, predictable and slavishly in thrall to the hydra-headed monsters of entertainment and consumption. Without it, we live as mere persons, not as spirits, guided through life by road maps prepared for us, not by others *per se,* but by a machinery of hellish otherness in which we, as persons, are hopelessly entangled.

ß

Enough of this. If I return to that mythical road in Kansas, I realise that my usual entry to Eluard's otherworld is to stumble upon it, on those rare occasions when I am not distracted by the usual business of existing: work, worry, being among others (*among*, that is, as opposed to *with*: Heidegger's distinction). I can pick out moments – lasting a few seconds at a time, to an hour, to a whole afternoon or night – when I have entered into that immediate otherworld and, though there is no narrative attached to such incidents that allows for a retelling, I find myself returning, again and again, to memories that I cannot share with others, or fully pin down for myself. Which, in one sense, is a perfect description of the lyric poem: another point of entry to the quotidian, another source of that clarity of being that alchemists call *pleroma*. At its best, the lyric opens a door in the everyday and allows me to pass into the otherworld behind the taken-for-granted; this art is not therapeutic as such, yet it is an attempt – on the part of the poet and possibly, at the moment of composition, purely for his or her own sake – to heal the imagination. "Metaphors are the means by which the oneness of the world is poetically brought about," says Hannah Arendt; and healing could fairly be described as an attempt at oneness, a renewal of the connection to the continuum of the real, a discipline for happiness.

Assume that the most common malady of contemporary life (in the 'developed' world, at least) is the sensation that the self is stolen away on a daily basis, that we are always struggling to win it back and, with it, to win back the perspective by which the quotidian may be experienced in its fullness. Meanwhile, what – if anything – is *visible* of the subject is a false self, a public construct resulting from a process of invention with which, to a greater or lesser extent, we ourselves collaborate. ("The light of the public darkens everything", Heidegger says.) If this is so, the task is to break that false self and move into Eluard's otherworld, the *true* Kingdom of Heaven. The reading of a lyric poem thus becomes a magical rite that re-enacts the process of being lost on the road, a radical illumination of the real world and a revelation of the living self, for a moment made visible in its true substance. I am not talking about analogy here: stumbling out of the engineered mundane into the (God-)given quotidian may be a matter of luck or chance, while the making of a poem is at least partly a matter of skill and discipline; but, at its best, the lyric offers the same radical illumination that chance affords us when we wander off the map. For poetry works where maps are useless: like a passport, the lyric allows us to enter the otherworld, but it is neither road map nor field guide. Upon arrival in Eluard's Kingdom, all we have is imagination and the difficult leap of trusting our own (many) senses; over there, we are not who we are in our public lives, but being there is how we come to be revealed.

ß

The question of visibility is crucial. Children become distinct persons by being seen; what generates attention is repeated, refined, prized. By the same token, to deny someone his or her visibility is to deny them existence: they continue to be, at least for a time, but *not being attended to*, not being seen and heard, leads to a form of sadness only otherwise observed in domestic animals. Obviously, this is not a question of *actual* (in)visibility; it is a matter of the radical self who *sees* the illumined world being systematically excluded from social discourse. It takes the patience – or the perversity – of a saint to live alone in a state of grace; the rest of us want to speak about that bourne from which we have, miraculously, returned. Or rather, not to speak, but to sing. It will seem, more often than not, that our off-map experiences are utterly private and beyond communication. But this is the paradox of poetry: the private event that illumines the poet's world is recreated and re-navigated, privately, by the reader; but the medium by which that event must be conveyed is a public one. In order to make a poem, we must subvert, not language itself, but the way language is used to consolidate social convention, just as, in order to become visible as we truly are, we must surrender our visibility as public – and so authorised – persons, in a world that is entirely of our own making.

This is all theory, of course. All abstraction. What I really want to talk about is the Midwest, where radical change can happen at any moment. The Midwest is a land of storms and floods, a land of big rivers and hurricanes and earthquakes (no wonder the Old Testament is so popular there). The Midwest is so open to the sky that everything under that wide roof seems provisional. Houses are built, not to withstand nature, but for ease of re-assembly, after they have been blown, or washed, or shaken to pieces. This is reflected in the stories that this land tells: in the English heartland's classic fantasy of entering *l'autremonde*, Alice falls, rather gently, out of the Oxford landscape and lands, quite softly, in an otherworld that, like Hades, is entirely underground (she is, in fact, a modern Proserpine, or – given Carroll's marriage fantasies – Eurydice). In *The Wizard of Oz*, however, Dorothy is literally blown away: entry to the other world is only vouchsafed by an act of violence, and the intense stillness that comes thereafter.

The two stories have many parallels: both the Alice and Oz books have a central, *active* female character; both introduce us to a world where the normal rules do not apply, a world whose characters are (like the girls themselves) wilful and unpredictable – natural forces, rather than persons as such. In both stories, there are moments of extraordinary stillness; both heroines are granted insights that cannot be obtained by reason, in spite of the fact that both try, doggedly, to apply the logic of the mundane world to situations that are beyond comprehension. The one significant difference (other than the more obvious moral content of the Oz books) is that Alice falls into her otherworld as if falling into a sleep (and, returning from that world, she is quick to dismiss it as a dream), whereas Dorothy is not so easily convinced that the otherworld is insubstantial, perhaps because the event that took her there was so very powerful and the forces with which she had to contend were so very perverse. Dorothy recognises that entry to such a world is an immense gift: it is also a means by which she can renew the landscape that Aunt Em and Uncle Henry inhabit. In the closing pages, rather than being dismissed as a dream, the cyclone is seen as the (re-)entry point to a fuller appreciation of the quotidian:

> "The Silver Shoes," said The Good Witch, "have wonderful powers. And one of the most curious things about them is that they can carry you to any place in the world in three steps, and each step will be made in the wink of an eye. All you have to do is knock the heels together three times and command the shoes to carry you wherever you wish to go."
>
> "If that is so," said the child, joyfully, "I will ask them to carry me back to Kansas at once."

Naturally, her wish is granted, but there is enough in the detail of her return for the reader to guess that her perspective has changed:

> Instantly she was whirling through the air, so swiftly that all she could see or feel was the wind whistling past her ears. The Silver Shoes took but three steps, and then she stopped so suddenly that she rolled over on the grass several times before she knew where she was. At length, however, she sat up and looked about her.
>
> "Good gracious!" she cried. For she was sitting on the broad Kansas prairie, and just before her was the new farmhouse Uncle Henry had built after the cyclone had carried away the old one.

At which point Aunt Em comes out to water the cabbages and sees Dorothy "running towards her". All these details – the cows, the cabbages, Dorothy rolling on the grass – are ordinary and familiar, yet they are transformed by the child's experiences in Oz, of which she speaks "gravely" (an echo, perhaps, of the "gray" that was so prevalent in the first chapter, but also a transformation from that Gradgrindly existence to a first glimmer of joyful sagacity). What matters, here, is not Dorothy's sojourn in Oz, so much as the manner of her return, a journey into the quotidian that, like the fairy stories Baum invokes in his introduction, *renews* the familiar, as much as it offers 'escape' from the restrictions imposed by convention. The otherworld is seen to exist, but it isn't Oz, it's here, enfolded in *celui-là*.

ॐ

Let us précis. For now, I am using the term *the quotidian* to mean the actual unfolding of the world around us, the 'out-there' of it, the kingdom-at-hand. Set against that is *the banal*. The banal is what we make of the quotidian when imagination fails: a condition that can arise from fatigue, dislocation, need, or simply as the result of 'socialisation'. The quotidian is the lyric poet's grail: the otherworld so carefully folded within the taken-for-granted as to be almost invisible. One glimpse of that otherworld can be the making of a lyric poem – and, by extension, another step towards *pleroma*.

In the Midwest, it seems to me, the *celui-là* is very thin. The earth is open to the sky, the land is wide and self-similar for hundreds of miles and there are moments when the world seems empty, or as the American poet Allison Funk puts it, in the final section of her third book, *The Knot Garden*:

> Nothing. Nothing again.
> Its dominion.

This closing section, entitled *In the Heartland*, distils into eleven beautiful lyric poems the argument about Midwestern poetry that I am pursuing here; and I want to linger over them for a moment. As it happens, Allison Funk is not *from* the Midwest: she was born in Delaware and her early work reflects those origins; yet, from her second collection, *Living at the Epicenter*, onwards, she has consistently engaged, not only with a Midwestern landscape (she now lives near St Louis) but also with the drama of entry – often by way of some violent or traumatic event – into the stillness of Eluard's *autremonde*. Other poets have explored that drama, but Funk's perspective is highly individual and her work – clear, unshowy, questioning – is as fine as anything being written now in its invocation of the quiet after the storm, where the kingdom-at-hand shines through, sometimes overwhelming in its immediacy, sometimes only just hinted at, a fleeting clue to the possibility of a fuller self in a wider world – as in another *Heartland* poem, 'Appearance at Dusk', where the speaker encounters a deer that

> disturbed the equilibrium
> of dusk so little as she passed,
> I doubted the murky air
>
> had moved at all.

Yet, when the animal sees her, she is amazed by what happens:

> This time fixing me
> with a gaze that left me fallow.
>
> I don't know how she put to rest
> everything that eddied within me, how
> as long as we kept one another in sight
>
> windfall could have given way
> to snowfall beyond us.

The animal encounter is a common enough phenomenon in American poetry, but I can think of no other poet whose *dramatis personae* display such tenderness towards the natural world, even when they find it threatening or unsettling. The delicacy of the handling here, along with the deftness of the conclusion, mark 'Appearance at Dusk' as something extraordinary, reconciling, as it does, the sense of personal difficulty with fleeting entry into the otherworld (which belongs, so perfectly, to the deer):

> Delicious – summer, summer again
>
> amid the terror, evenings and mornings
> when I'd scare, when I would have bolted
> if love hadn't held me there.

Everything works beautifully here, in an understated way: the surprise of the word "terror", the ambiguity written into "scare", the reversal implied in "bolted" and the sudden, disconcerting appearance of that unexpected "love" in the last line (love for what? for whom?).

Yet this is an everyday encounter, common enough in any landscape. A more specifically Midwestern example of the sudden revelation of a divine, yet troubling, quotidian appears a few pages later, in 'On the Prairie', whose subject is the fine haze of cottonwood down that blows across the land in late summer:

> Look down at your feet
>   or straight ahead
> as you walk
>   and you easily miss them,

the poem begins; and to begin with it is hard to see where this will go, other than in some conventional 'nature poem' direction. The revelation – the giddy fall into the otherworld – only comes towards the end, when the poet has misled us into thinking we really have taken up residence in the picturesque:

> looking up now I'm having trouble
>
> distinguishing them
>   from the clouds on an updraft
> they're floating towards.
>   I cannot trust my sight.
>
> This has happened before,
>   hasn't it? Is always always
>
> happening. If only I heard a tintinnabulum,
>   the smallest tinkling bell
>
> ringing when something's real
>   so I would know;
> if I could hold, just for a moment,
>   what spirits this close –
>
> but caught,
>   and in my damp palm,
> what was like unto a breeze,
>   what-I-would-be
>
> sticks,
>   even when I say go,
> sally forth, it stays, will not, little soul
>   of mine, ghost.

In one sense, nothing could be slighter than this haze of cottonweed seed, yet it is not the event so much as the fact of noticing it, and discovering in the noticing that, not only has it happened before, but it is always happening – this kingdom-at-hand, this otherworld – and the self that goes with it, the "what-I would-be" is always there, even if it is marked by the poignancy of that wish to be alerted to the real that it keeps missing, and by the fact that it cannot "sally forth" (a sly touch, that hint of willow) but "sticks".

The stillest moment and the most direct experience of *l'autremonde* in the *Heartland* series comes, however, in the brief and deceptively simple-seeming 'Afterward':

> Amid the debris,
> the wreckage of events,
> it was somehow as unbroken
> in its way
> as the egg found in the rubble
> of a leveled house
> or, under the dust
> that was someone's good china
> once, the teacup
> rimmed in gold leaf,
> a baby unearthed
> alive, or most surprising perhaps,
> in working order
> the chimes of the quarter hour
> a man heard standing atop a staircase
> leading nowhere:
> *amid the debris, a little melody*
> rung against something bigger,
> louder, the megaphone of the twister,
> the line she would sing to herself.

Here, in a poem that links back to the beautiful, hushed title sequence of Funk's *Living at the Epicenter* (an "afterward" to that book, as well as to the events it now describes) the poet brings together the essential ingredients of the *autremonde* encounter: the violent event, in this case "the twister"; the breakdown of the given order; the miraculous quiet of *afterward*, where the music of what happens in the other world – a melody, a line – suggests itself to the persona (note that, in spite of that "in working order", the clock itself is not mentioned, only "the chimes of the quarter hour"); the staircase that leads nowhere; the sense one has that everything, not just space but also time, has changed, but that this change, an acknowledged catastrophe in *the banal*, is a potentially mind-changing revelation in the quotidian. In this sense, 'Afterward' can be seen as a template of how to read Funk's *Heartland* poems, each of which is an encounter with the quotidian that leads both persona and reader, if not always to the abandonment, at least to a reconsideration, of the banal.

Perhaps the most powerful of Funk's considerations of cataclysmic events, however, is that central title sequence in *Living at the Epicenter*. This sequence of five short lyrics takes its cue from Eliza Bryan "of New Madrid,

Missouri, [who] wrote one of the few surviving accounts of the series of earthquakes that shook the region in late 1811 and 1812". The first of these is a fractured, impressionistic telling of the earthquake itself:

> Oaks thrusting at one another,
>   the houses come unfastened.
>   Heaved from their nests
>
> birds land
>   on her shoulders and head.
> Wings in her face.
>   Odor of sulfur.

Here is the cataclysmic event, recalled in language that, while neither archaic nor overly Biblical, recalls the vocabulary of Eliza Bryan's time, with its references to "a babel of trees", the brutish sexuality of the "Mississippi / like an animal in heat" and that satanic hint of sulphur noted above. Here, and in the second poem (where the river runs backwards), we are in the world of conventional order, though only for long enough to watch that order being torn apart. Yet already, even in that second lyric, there is a glimpse of something more, a fleeting yet telling hint of the quotidian:

>   a lady and six children
>   all lost.
> Flatboat, raft, all the tenuous breaths,
>   the young cottonwoods
>   broken with such regularity
>
> from a distance
>   they might look like a work of art.

This poem closes with its protagonist able to see, though only "as if underwater"; soon, however, the third poem has her "stumbling miles / waist deep in blood warm water" – the shattering of her world is not yet finished, and she will not be ready to enter an *autremonde* that is as terrifying as it is miraculous until everything she knows and trusts, everything she has taken for granted, is broken:

> When she holds out her arms
>   to the children
>
> silt runs through her fingers.
>   Borderless,
> nothing's familiar.
>   Yard, road.
>   Others, self.

It is a terrible moment, yet this is the point at which she enters the continuum of the quotidian, the point at which the mapped world fails her and she cannot tell herself apart, quite, from what surrounds her. It has, it seems, taken this cataclysm for her – and for us – to see that the logic by which we live, day to day, is only a subset of a wider, more mysterious order. In the fourth poem, the woman recovers her memory "like a fever" and begins looking back, searching for the signs that should have warned her of the impending disaster, remembering blighted crops, hailstones,

> passenger pigeons
> arriving suddenly
>
> like the Pharaoh's locusts, swarming
> in the fields, hundreds in a single tree.

With hindsight, she sees that the signs were there: the animals knew and, had she but known how to read the world about her, she would have guessed what was coming from the "grey squirrels in thousands / drowned trying to cross the river". Finally, in a moment that echoes Casca's "civil strife in heaven" speech in *Julius Caesar*, she upbraids herself for being so out of tune with the auguries:

> How was it she didn't see it coming,
>   she asks herself,
> remembering the eclipse
>   of the moon, autumn's comet
>   and the monster born between its legs.

The final poem opens with another animal image, as:

> A great blue heron
>   starts up out of the wetlands slowly,
> looking broken at first,
>   long legs trailing
>   before, heavy winged, it flies.

"Another sign, she thinks", but of what? After such upheaval, the world can never be the same again: or rather, she, this woman, can never go back to the world-taken-for-granted where she once lived. All she can do now is write, trying to make sense of events and, in so doing,

                    tell
            what she's learned:

        how in the middle of one night
            the world we've known
        can open up without warning,
            all of nature
                begin speaking in tongues.

Here the poem ends, quietly, with both protagonist and poet setting pen to paper, each determined to "tell / what she's learned", the former from the event itself, the latter from bringing together a reading of Eliza Bryan's account of the earthquake with the unspecified private events that have brought her to the contemplation of a new self, born from the wreckage of given expectations into a world that is both more dangerous and, at the same time (with that image of the broken heron mending itself in flight and that frightening, yet liberating idea of nature "speaking in tongues"), more miraculous than she could ever have imagined – till now.

                    ℬ

Some time after that drive in the Flint Hills, on another highway, a thousand miles from Kansas, I came across the same turning, the same country road, the same glimmers of cottonwood down drifting across the fields. I noticed it immediately and, turning off the highway, I drove for twenty miles or so till the track fizzled out in a sandy wash, a line of willows, a silence broken now and then by the call of a red-winged blackbird, crouched amongst the reeds. It was a warm, egg-blue and straw-coloured afternoon, and I was nowhere in particular; but that's the thing about *l'autremonde:* it turns up in the most unlikely places, and when you least expect it, looking just like the *celui-là.*

Silent in Darien:

The San Blas Islands, Panama

HENRY SHUKMAN

The engines of the little plane moan in boredom as we duck through air pockets, climbing over the central mountains of the Isthmus of Panama. Ahead, emerging from the limit of vision, a silver sheet stretches away from the green jigsaw of headlands: the Caribbean Sea. From this height it looks like beaten silver, dotted with little cloud-shadows, a leopard-skin sea every bit as startling as Balboa's first glimpse of the Pacific in 1516 (it wasn't stout Cortes after all), famously celebrated in Keats's sonnet. That glimpse occurred only a few miles away, in the mountains that we're flying over.

In fact the stippling of shadows are islands, little fragments of coconut heaven littered along Panama's north-eastern coast. The San Blas Islands, or better islets – they're never more than half a mile wide, and some are cartoon islands supporting one solitary palm – are a territory unto themselves. Their inhabitants are the 20,000 Cuna Indians. In 1925 the Cunas revolted in a mini-war of independence, only quelled by the intervention of America, uneasy at the prospect of armed dispute so close to its canal. The result was Kuna Yala, their autonomous region, where they live the old way, on fish and rice, with machetes and dugouts, bamboo and coconut longhouses, matriarchal rules and puberty rites for girls celebrated not with home brew but home chew – sugar cane beer fermented with saliva. It might be the last intact piece of pre-Columbian Caribbean, the very world that Columbus, Cortes and Nuñez de Balboa found paddling up to their caravels when they first hove in sight.

No one comes here. I'm only coming because an American magazine heard about it and thought a British poet might like to take a look at the origins of a famous image of English poetry. There are no maps of San Blas. What would you want one for? Each island is walkable in a matter of minutes, in some cases seconds (as long as the heat hasn't debilitated you) and they lie so close to one another that the neighbouring ones are always visible. Few outsiders sail their waters, which are laced with reefs (and with the half-rotted skeletons of vessels that tried). It's a lost sea, lying silent in Darien true enough, last wilderness of Central America, the only point between Alaska and Tierra del Fuego that no highway can cross, the missing link in the American chain.

I first heard about the Cuna from reading Levi-Strauss, founding father of structural anthropology. In his seminal essay, 'The Efficacy of Symbols', he describes how when a Cuna woman is having trouble in child-birth the shaman chants a myth about a hero battling down to the underworld, negotiating with various spirits, then fighting his way back. By the time he gets home, the woman has invariably given birth (hence the title of the essay).

Yet the Cuna know about the other side too. Many have worked in Panama City and the 'Zone' (the Canal Zone). They see a few tourists, they have stores stocked with coke and cigarettes, albeit usually just one brand. (One shop I wandered into had stacks and stacks of cartons on high shelves. 15,000 cigarettes, I worked out, and every one of them a Menthol Doral.)

As soon as I step off the little plane, I ride in a dugout to Chichimen, island of the *chichi*, a small plum-like fruit. The island's not more than 400 yards across, with a population of twenty, and lies a few miles out from the coast, on the fringe of Cuna territory. When the weather is clear, you see the khaki mountains of the mainland far away. Otherwise, they vanish in white haze. A reef lies half a mile beyond, last reef before the open sea, roaring constantly like a train.

The *jefe* of Chichimen is Don Ramon, who worked for twenty years as a chef in Panama City, then returned to claim his patrimony. He is a small old man with a permanent smile, and three sturdy pegs for teeth either side of an empty gum.

"I haven't left this island in seventeen years," he told me. "Not a single day. My father died, I came straight back. All my brothers have gone too now," he says, raising a hand from his cane. "I'm the last." *Soy el ultimo.*

He may be the last but he is not alone. His niece Buna lives in the hut next door, a middle-aged woman with the Beatle-bob and constant smile of Cuna women, and in a third hut across the yard lives Muchacho, "Boy," her estranged husband. Boy rides a dugout like something out of The-Flintstones-At-The-Beach, a hefty bole with a sizable shark-bite taken out of the stern and a lump of lava for an anchor. Every morning he shoves it down the beach off its log roller and paddles into the lagoon, pausing to bail with half a cracked gourd every few minutes. You see him bobbing out there near the reef as the sun climbs up. When he paddles back in late morning, another member of the island entourage, Eulogio, comes to the beach to meet him. Eulogio loads the fluttering snappers into a broken clock-face that must have once washed up with a tide. (One of the Cuna's storehouses is the sea, the Walmart of the Waves.)

Boy would like to live with his wife Buna but she won't have him. But Eulogio, who shares her hut, is not the reason why. Cuna have clear-cut dress codes. Men wear shorts or trousers, women wear wraps (*molas*) and blouses and habitually daub bright rouge on their cheeks. Eulogio, a youngish man with long wavy hair, uses the rouge, wears a pink singlet and wraps a towel round his waist, a halfway house to a woman's wrap. For he is not a man but an *omegit*, a man-woman, a Cuna transvestite. It doesn't occur to the Cuna not to accept that some boys gravitate towards women's things – needle and thread, the cooking hut, the babies. They make no attempt to get them to conform. They don't disapprove. They allow these men to grow up as *omegits* because that's how they are. They say the *omegits* make the best *molas*.

Eulogio, Chichimen's *omegit*, carries the catch to the cooking hut behind Don Ramon's house. Ramon sits in his doorway watching the goings-on. Soon Buna will put more coconut stems on the fire and start deep-frying the fish for lunch, or else will heap up the coconut husks and smoke the fish.

Meanwhile a fifth friend, Señor José, is hard at work grating copra to make coconut milk for the rice. (No rice is decent without a generous splash of it.) Having grated up a bowlful he ladles in some well water (wherever you dig on the island you find water) and inserts his mahogany hands in the pulp, squeezing the mix through a perforated gourd, making the rich white juice flood out.

Señor José is Ramon's age, bow-legged and light-headed. Every evening he comes past my hut with a raggedy towel over his shoulder and announces that he is on his way to the well to wash. "It's good to wash in the evening," he declares, toppling on his stiff legs. "In the evening *and* in the morning," he adds.

Four dogs live in the compound too: the puppy Suzuki, the barker Negra, of whom they agree that she's a *buena watchiman*, and Tambourin, an elegant young bitch who likes to sleep under my hammock. The fourth "dog" is Achu, which means Dog, although in fact he's a young man. His name causes peals of laughter each time it is uttered. No one will tell me how he earned it.

♫

The weird thing about living in all this nature is how it reminds you of cities. First there's that industrial noise from the reef – a constant resonance in the back of the skull. Then this house I'm staying in – it's a palm shelter with only one wall, a kind of gazebo in which to sling your hammock, opening onto a grove of coconuts that lead down to the sea some fifteen yards away. With the drifting shade of the fronds, it feels just like a pillared patio, and has a sense of proportion, an inbuilt calm, that an architect would die to create. And the sea just here is swimming-pool green, and comes round the side of the island in a warm channel four feet deep and maybe ten yards wide, before the bottom rises further out in coral heads and underwater grasses. It's like a dream pool, always clean, naturally plumbed and filtered and heated, just at the end of the patio.

I look straight out to that roaring reef. Sometimes you see the black faces of breakers rising like shark fins above the horizon, then unfurling like mirages. (There are no real sharks in Kuna Yala. Long ago a shaman turned himself into one and lured them all away, then devised a metaphysical fence to keep them out. So far none have penetrated it. Nor do hurricanes ever come here: the Cunas beat pans and shout when one is threatening to approach. A hurricane is a wind that has lost its way. When it hears them it can get its bearings again.) All around lies broad sea, with a dozen or so distant islands jumbled on the skyline in smoky-blue, murky-grey, deep-green.

You fall asleep with the wind stirring the folds of your hammock and the thunder of the reef resonating at the deepest pitch of hearing like infrared sound.

༘

Only the pots, machetes and I are intruders in this mesolithic paradise. It's a wonderful thing to live in the midst of nature and natural things, but it's hard to say exactly why. Something happens. At first you just feel: this is a nice place. Then, after a day or two, you find a warmth has spontaneously arisen within. The first night, sleeping in the open wind, is a stirring, restless experience, but you wake at dawn excited and ready to give yourself to the island. You will walk round it, explore, maybe go fishing with Boy or Achu.

Is there any phrase that holds a greater promise than *explore the island?* You can't help but imagine living here. What it would do for you... All your reasoned defences melting in the heat, nature entering your mind and body, performing its subtle surgery, relieving you of the ability to worry. Then you think: why *not* stay? Why *not* live like this? Perhaps there's really nothing stopping you. You could enter the old dream of harmony, where conscious and subconscious melt into one. Life here is one deep dream of easy motion. The rock of the dugout, the swing of the hammock, the glitter of palm fronds, the scintillations of the lagoon – nothing stops moving. As if the world had become a great lung filled with a rhythmic breathing.

You walk around your domain: so isolated, so protected. You may never have felt this safe. You begin to notice patterns everywhere: in the stars of the palms fronds; in the pelicans' endlessly repeated glide and plunge, glide and plunge; in the little grasses that sprout up in long straight rows off buried roots; in the starred perforations of a sand dollar. You begin to wish you too could be infused with a similar patterning, then realise that you are, you're just unschooled in seeing it. The veil of civilization tears. Beneath, you glimpse a man who would take pleasure in beaching his own dugout, in hanging up a bleached board he found washed up on the beach to serve as a shelf. In bailing his craft with a gourd. In fuelling his own fire, cooking his catch.

Yet each morning in the fishing dug-out your fingers reek of death: of fish oil, fish blood.

The pleasure here is akin to the model railway: seeing a complete world intact, replete with its spirits and Creator and ancestral sages, its coconut currency (they come in bunches of four tied at the stems) and its own indigenous technology. It is woven of a single fabric, the palm.

Panama may be a banana republic, but this is a coconut culture. A handful of ways to use the palm:

1. Drink the nut's water.
2. Eat the fresh copra.
3. Chip off a piece of husk for use as a spatula.
4. Smoke fish over the dried husks.
5. Grate, soak and sieve the copra for coconut milk.
6. Grate, heat and skim to get coconut oil:
    a. for frying,
    b. for lamps,
    c. for skin lotion.
7. Burn old palm-stems for firewood.
8. Weave fronds for roofing.
9. Lop trunks for house-posts.
10. Roll logs for wheeling dugouts into water.
11. Strip spines off the fronds and tie together for brooms.
12. Lie in the trees' shade.

Then you get *the rash*. Even here a little rain must fall.

ॐ

Achu takes me fishing. We paddle out, tipping alarmingly in his log. Water seeps in around the tin patches that have been nailed over the leaks and around the nail heads in the patches. Every few minutes one of us has to stop paddling and bail.

The reef's roar grows louder. A hundred yards off, Achu ties his yellow rope to his anchor rock and chucks it over the side. We bait our hooks with the little *sardinas* we caught earlier off the beach and start dangling for snappers and young parrotfish. After a few lost bites Achu dons his mask and performs a curious lolloping headfirst exit, developed specifically for use in precarious dugouts, and disappears with his snare in search of lobster.

He is away a long time. Now and then I see a distant head bobbing in the water. I carry on fishing, missing bite after bite, working my way through the bait. The wind seems to pick up. Achu told me there were two winds here, *brisas* off the sea and *viento* from the land. Today, being the third day after the new moon, the wind is supposed to change from sea to land, which would mean quieter water. So far he seems to be wrong. The rippled lagoon is becoming choppy. I begin to appreciate the full implications of the dugout: it really is just a log, eminently rollable. I bail like mad but the water keeps coming in. Every time a wavelet slaps our prow, a jet of foam spurts through a knot-hole in the wood.

And the sun is high now. The gathering breeze keeps me cool, but I am taking a lot of rays on my unacclimatized limbs and cranium.

By the time Achu returns and we paddle back to the beach I feel distinctly light-headed. I follow the path through the palms back to our hut and swing myself in the hammock. Achu was right: the wind has shifted to the land now. At last I understand why mine is the only house on the northern shore. Here, in the lee of all the palms of the interior, the breeze dies completely. Which means it's fantastically hot, as if the very ground were red-hot iron. Moreoever, all the insects Pandora freed wake from their sleep. I slap six dreamy mosquitoes on my legs in as many seconds. Horseflies circle my head. Tiny house-flies dart round my face. Now and then a sharp prick has me searching leg or arm, where I find a mere crumb of life smaller than a sand-grain, that crumbles under my attempts to brush it away – far too small, one would think, to deliver such a sharp stab. I sweat; I itch. I fan at the marauders. The hut becomes an entomologist's fantasy.

There's only one safe place: the swimming channel off the beach. I run down just in time to see a large dugout filled with a family from a neighbouring island come sailing by, the sail a collection of rags stitched together. They all stare at me with fixed bewilderment. Bashfulness gets the better of me. I return to the hut, wrap in a sheet, pray for wind.

ℬ

Buna and Eulogio bring over the evening meal: an aluminium pan of rice and plantains; an old frisbee serving as a platter for the fried fish. Buna greets me with her usual smile, puts down her load, then raises her eyebrows, emits a whoop of surprise, and takes hold of my arm.

I had not noticed, but it is covered from wrist to bicep in an angry rash. The other arm too, and now that I take a look my legs have also been colonized. Sunburn? Salt rash? Prickly heat? Some medley of insect venoms?

Whether the rash worsens or just seems to, now that I'm aware of it, the cocktail of sun, salt, insect and rash works up a head of discomfort. And a storm approaches. After supper I sit on the beach watching the lightning's display a few islands away. Out of the black sky sudden cloudscapes of gold and mauve erupt. Half a minute later long grumbles interfere with the even roar of the reef.

It is quite a storm. It spreads either way round the island, embracing it. Clatters of firecrackers fall down the sky. I retreat to my hammock. Minute by minute the flashes encompass more and more of the sky, the thunderclaps intensify. The wind drops completely. For five minutes all is quiet: a sickly overheated lull. Then suddenly the wind is racing in, sucking through the open hut, hissing in the palms. The rain arrives with apocalyptic decisiveness. It's not long before the thatch gives way, dribbling onto my face in the dark. I cocoon myself in the hammock. I haven't been this scared of a storm since I was a child camping in the garden. I feel as breakable as bamboo. The thunderbolts shake the wicker frame of my chest. The wind flaps around my balsa-wood legs.

The wind dies but lightning flickers silently long into the night.

In the morning Achu pays a visit. He sweeps back his long hair and says what a storm, what *relampagos*. "Luz-*boom!* Luz-*boom!*" he says, in case I don't know what *relampagos* are, throwing his hands apart like an explosion on each *boom!*

ß

The next day help for the rash arrives in the form of Henry Harrison. Henry, a Cuna who speaks a garbled English half-remembered from his years in the Zone, arrives with two companions from El Porvenir in a dugout with a small engine. They are all on their way to Rio Tigre, an island half way to Colombia, some fifty miles away.

He wears thick glasses and slacks, a shirt with a breast pocket from which protrudes a biro cap: the garb of the intellectual. Henry is conducting "investigations" into his people.

"Yeah when I eight I got a big dream, a man with a beard come tell me I live to a hundred and meet peoples from all over the world. Then a cargo boat take me to Panama. I cry and cry, and that really happen you know." His conversation skips nimbly from autobiography to native philosophy and back. Henry has visited most of the Cuna islands and knows his people well. He draws me into his friend Don Ramon's hut and launches into a speech on the wisdom of the Cuna healers. Before he jumps onto some other topic, I jump first, presenting him with my left arm. Does he know of a healer who could help my rash?

Indeed. Rio Tigre, where he's going, happens to be home to the best Cuna healers.

It's hard to leave Chichimen. The island has become a place of gestation, a *cuna* or cradle. But soon the waves have taken hold of my dreaminess. As we tip and loll through the waters, the many islands trundle back and forth like beetles along the horizon, rearranging themselves so just when you think you know which is Achutupo, which Corbiski, you realise you no have idea at all. The mountains of the mainland move closer, fuming like an old fire.

℘

We coast up to Rio Tigre's dock and suddenly it's like arriving in the middle of Chapter 14 of a Graham Greene novel. A dilapidated Colombian boat creaks at the dock, draped with supine peddlars from Barranquilla taking siestas amid piles of knick-knacks and vegetables. A concrete quay gives onto a concrete plaza where four or five individuals rest in the thin shade of eaves. A young woman, a friend of Henry's, charges me three dollars in "island tax."

We idle away the afternoon in a shop, drinking orange sodas, then in the school teacher's house, swinging in hammocks.

When darkness falls Henry conducts me to the Congress House to see the *sahila*, or chief. In the twilight of the giant longhouse two men at the front sway side by side in white hammocks. One keeps up a stream of high-pitched emphatic chanting, punctuated every so often by a decisive note from the other: *Nabiri! Nabiri!*

"He is telling for the history of Cuna peoples and cultures," Henry informs me, making no attempt to keep his voice down. I realise that quite a number of men seated on the rows of benches maintain a low babble of chatter. Apparently no one is expected to listen too closely to the lengthy recitation going on. The sweet smell of tobacco fills the room. A hurricane lamp hangs in one corner, making the whole scene tender with its weak light.

A man with a belly – rare here – slouches on a bench at the front. On seeing Henry and me he leans over and reaches through the hammock strings to shake hands. Henry and he start talking, ignoring the solemnities a few feet away. Then Henry tells me this is the *sahila* and I may present my petition. "He speak Espanny," he lets me know.

I get a sudden attack of shyness. There are a lot of men in the room, and more keep arriving. I am in their meeting-house. An old man nearby, his face glistening like walnut wood in the light of the lamp, stuffs his pipe full of aromatic tobacco and lights up, softly sucking, half-listening for what I will have to say for myself.

After a greeting elaborate enough to make a courtier of the *Siglo de Oro* blush, I express my hope that I may be treated by one of his village's renowned *curanderos*.

He speaks to Henry, and Henry says to me, "OK, OK, let's go."

I get up and follow him into a street riddled with puddles from rain earlier. "So you haves to pay three dollars and you can't carry photograph," he says. "We go in the morning for seven clocks, eight clocks."

ℬ

In the morning an old woman with a giant gold nose-ring and a wrinkled face holds my arm over a metal bowl full of a black liquid like cold coffee. She scoops up one palmful after another, bathing my arm in it. It feels cooling, like camphor. The itch I woke up with disappears.

We are in the yard between a cooking-hut and a longhouse. The woman's grandson stares at me from behind a pink toy plate with which he shields his face. I can see he's grinning. He is two and a half years old, and a special child. He is already a shaman. Shamans are born not made. They come into the world possessed of such power that their mothers invariably die in childbirth. Shamans grow faster than other children. By three they can already talk like adults. By ten they know the properties of the many medicinal plants on the mainland. They eat and drink more than other kids. This boy looks like a typical Cuna six-year-old.

He, along with a little crowd of other family members, is watching his grandmother at work on me. She grins and lets out satisfied grunts as the black fluid trickles down my arms. Occasionally she chats to me in Cuna and one of her sons, a man in shorts and an orange baseball cap, translates into Spanish.

"This medicine is very strong," he says. "If it touch your tongue it kill you dead. You have to wash your hands before eating."

I have had no breakfast and am relieved that this lotion seems to be the extent of the curing session. I had imagined a long smoky séance.

Then the old woman brings out a glass of *chicha*, a nonalcoholic maize drink. It's for me, a cool milky glass half full of milled corn husks. The real session has in fact yet to begin. We all troop into the longhouse, where the old woman conducts me to a hammock. Against the bamboo wall beside it are piled the accoutrements of the shaman's art: gourds full of dried roots, powders, rocks, a box of hollow flutes, knives and pots and, most conspicuous of all, an entourage of *neles*, the wooden dolls which assist shamans in their work. They range in size from five inches to five feet, and all wear little bowler hats and have simple Mr Men faces. Spirits live in them. When the wood gets old and splits you know the spirit has left. Some have red paint on their cheeks, indicating they are female.

The old woman's husband, Don Ignacio, is a shaman. He brings in a little pile of hot coals on a palm stem and tips them on the sand floor. Then he fetches a gourd of white cocoa beans. He starts chanting. A sticky oppressive heat fills this longhouse. Its ceiling must be too low. It is untidy too – children's cast-off clothes, old crisp packets, plastic toys, litter the floor. The old man's singing suddenly seems to become clearer. My ears prick up. His voice is pure and sharp like a boy's. He starts dropping the cocoa beans on his bed of coals. A strong, bitter smoke fills our corner of the house. The smoke is the incense on which the *neles* feed. He is nourishing them for the work ahead.

He gives my hammock a push. I swing gently, lulled by the motion and by his voice. At one point he opens up a hardcover ledger. Inside, over the margins and lines, someone has painted rows of symbols, some hiero-glyphic-like, others paintings of animal figures done in bright, strong watercolours. Don Ignacio and his troop of *neles*, I learn afterwards, have gone on a journey up a river to where the spirits live. It seems a spider-spirit stole some part of me and after much diplomacy, he persuaded the spider to return it.

I had always thought spiders were on our side in the war against insects.

Afterwards the sunlight seems yellow as egg-yolk, the sea blue like smoke. Ignacio's son Fidel, the widower father of the Divine Child who can already see the future, gives me a small wooden doll, which he tells me is called *Maniwite*: He Who Favours Money.

ß

It is an arduous two-day task to find boats back to Chichimen. I sit soaked in dugouts under the sun for long hours, propelled in turn by paddle, engine and ragged sail. There's nothing for it but to learn to let the rocking of the waves lull me like a hammock. It is a glorious silver evening when we scud into the lagoon between Chichimen and its neighbour. The coconut palms look wet, the sea green like fresh paint.

Don Ramon steps out of his hut to welcome me back. Buna, Eulogio and José laugh with delight when I step from the prow of the canoe, with my shoes on, straight into a deep wave. Buna and Eulogio pull up the cuffs of my shirt and start crowing over my arms: all gone, skin smoother than ever. The journey to Rio Tigre, the journey to these islands, the shaman's journey – for a moment all seem inseparable, with one shared object, apparent in my gleaming skin.

REVIEWS

The Listeners

ALISON BRACKENBURY

Glyn Maxwell, *The Sugar Mile*, Picador, £8.99, ISBN 0330438247
Nick Laird, *To a Fault*, Faber, £8.99, ISBN 0571223826

"It's Tate and Lyle, that's Tate and Lyle" – *The Sugar Mile*, Glyn Maxwell's book-long poem, sweetens when read, and heard, at length. It opens tentatively, in a New York bar, on 8 September 2001. A fashionable notebook (in the poet's hand), and deleted drafts (on the page), sent this listener into a spin of sour anxiety. But long poems often need scaffolding. The triumphant heart of *The Sugar Mile* is not New York but London, under bombing in the Blitz, where a grandmother calls upstairs:

> That was the thump you said. I got tea made
> Downstairs, oh my blessed back
> I swear. Let's have a look.

Here is Maxwell at his best, running the breaths and bluff of a living voice through a stanza whose art stays invisible. He is wise to turn, now, to the Second World War. His post-war generation has the privilege of distance, but the children of the bombing still speak. Maxwell echoes them, marvellously. Poetry is an awkward cousin, but at times she claims her place at history's table. "Give her a blanket for crying out loud the ghost girl".

The Blitz ghosts of *The Sugar Mile* live partly by the light of Maxwell's American perspective, and the successful haunting of his work by the boldness and freedoms of American poetry. His London voices, pattering to an audience of bombs, "that's Tate and Lyle's / one lump or two", are urgent but not simple. They are, as in the Blitz myth, stoic:

> I suppose we're 'refugees'.
> World's our oyster, Joey. Here,
> Help me with these.

But they are also, at times, implacably racist. The old man in the New York bar becomes the child mocked as "the ice-cream man [...] an eye-tie". The tough families have scarring secrets. The "ghost girl" keens to herself "crookback lodger [...] sly sly sly". Maxwell's mature technique, with its short, focused lines, its incantatory chants, is the scaffolding which upholds these voices' power. If connections flash into today's politics – "refugees" –

they draw their imaginative fire from the poem's complex life.

The Sugar Mile, perhaps like all extended work, is uneven. Some of the New York sections feel strained and confected. It is strange how the past drains the life from the present. But a long poem, like a book, should be judged by its best. At its peak, *The Sugar Mile* has the virtuosity and verve of vaudeville. Even the New York barman does his turn, spinning from the poet to underage customers.

> *Rum? What a wicked world.*
> *Sweetheart, you're gonna suffer. Okay try it.*

Writing the end of a long poem is often a nightmare. The Muse shrugs, leaving poets to their choices. Maxwell's solution is wit, neat but excluding, sweetened only by the memory that the poem is safe within it. *The Sugar Mile* richly rewards re-reading.

I have not seen a review of Maxwell's book in any newspaper I read. I have skimmed many pages about the excitement of new groups and their musics, some of which I think excellent. What is a poem's place, beside songs of such popularity and power? Should poets close their notebooks, and retire to the bar? No. Poetry is salvage. It does not need a studio, a synthesiser, or even a good voice. Mutter, and it is yours. Its rare meetings of thought, music and feeling flare in a dark fold of the mind that even a song cannot reach. Maxwell's best work is there.

Is Nick Laird's? Yes. The finest poems from his troubling and intriguing first collection leap into the mind. "Listen" commands the end of the penultimate poem, and Laird does listen; less to other voices, like Maxwell, than to landscapes and the turbulence of his own mind. 'Appendix', the final poem, catches the tone, with its almost perfect echo of a wind "*Hushing* our avenue's branches […] pitched closer to anger than wonder".

The violence of Laird's Ulster invades these poems. Its menace hums within the lines of 'Cuttings', in "the parking or calving or missing". In 'Oświęm', (Auschwitz), a whole poem ticks through honey's "amber tongue" and country stations to its final explosion: "bombs".

But Laird is a surprising poet. The quiet dairy herds of Ulster migrate to the landscape of "Imperial" Iraq. Before the Biblical lilt of war, "We are again among these ruins and the dying", sway the cows:

> pool-eyed and aware
> how close they come.

How close Laird brings the listener to a vast hinterland, where "the cattle lie down in each other's shelter". As an insight into enduring life, beyond war, and city, it is shamingly unusual.

The love poems of *To a Fault* encompass the brutal 'Aubade':

> Go home. I haven't slept alone
> in weeks –

They include a *tour de force* in 'Auction (no reserve)', which closes "waiting / willing. / Bid." Characteristically, this poem could equally well be about murder. Not so the wry 'To the Wife', which veers back from a vision of squinting old age to a time when

> all of the tunes are inside us and wordless.

Ruefully mature perspectives are one of the surprises of *To a Fault*. The urban bravado of drugs at the opening of 'Cycling through Snow –' is replaced by the decision (evading a glib final rhyme) to "freewheel home and slip inside". Mercifully, this is a poetry not even half in love with death. 'The Evening Forecast', in its tumble of couplets, measures, in insomnia, the rhythms of life:

> Everyone on earth is sleeping. I am the keel-scrape
>
> beneath their tidal breathing […]

Laird's formal range is as striking as his themes.

Any caveats? First collections often, in Keats's young phrase, show a "fine excess". Some of Laird's poems feel oddly constricted, by ponderous phrasing and truncated lines, as though they had been worked over by a writer immersed in prose. While brooding on this, I read the cover's announcement of a "debut novel". Prose and poetry are two hard horses to ride. Can it be done? Perhaps there will at least be time to return to love poems, and to the patience of cattle.

Alison Brackenbury's most recent collection is *Bricks and Ballads* (Carcanet, 2004). New poems can be seen at her website, www.alisonbrackenbury.co.uk.

War By Other Means

DAVID HERD

Christopher Logue, *Cold Calls: War Music continued*,
Faber and Faber, £8.99, ISBN 0571202772

Reviewing *All Day Permanent Red*, the previous instalment of Logue's Homer, in *Poetry Review* 93:2, Stephen Burt asked a question of Logue and Logue's subsequent reviewers. Would future books in the project, he wondered, as earlier books had done – Logue has been engaged in his adaptation of the *Iliad* on and off since the late fifties – succeed in "dramatising distinguishable characters in an articulate epic frame" ? This was not, as such, a criticism of *All Day Permanent Red*, which in its concentration on the battle scenes of books five to eight of the epic necessarily emphasized the rhythms of action over the tones of character. The point, rather, in the midst of the battle, was to remember that the *Iliad* isn't only a violent clash. With luck, Burt hoped, Logue would at some point turn his attention to Homer's book nine, in which, during a break in the action, and on the brink of defeat, Greek leaders – Nestor, Ajax, Odysseus and Patroclus among others – seek to persuade Achilles to rejoin the fray; to accept Agamemnon's apology and extravagant reparation for seizing Briseis (Achilles' "riband she", as Logue has it); to save his country, to bury his grudge.

So here we are:

Silence.

A ring of lights.

Within

Immaculate

In boat-cloaks lined with red

King Agamemnon's lords –

The depression of retreat,
The depression of returning to camp [...]

> 'King Agamemnon of Mycenae,
> God Called, God raised, God recognised,
> You are a piece of shit,' Diomed said.

Diomed is right. Or at least, Logue's Diomed is right about Logue's Agamemnon. "I was a fool," Agamemnon concedes ("wiping his eyes"), "[…] to take the she. // I shall pay fitting damages. Plus her, I offer him / The Corfiot armour that my father wore". This is all wrong. It sounds alright, promising even; Agamemnon acknowledging his mistake and making it clear that he is willing to make good. But Logue understands leadership, hears the self-aggrandizement in leadership's seeming contrition, and so has Agamemnon begin his speech not with "I was wrong" but "I was a fool", has him repeat the personal pronoun at least once too often. The trouble with Agamemnon, as Logue communicates deftly and with minimal recourse to commentary, is that he just can't keep himself out of it. He's like the leader who will go so far as to acknowledge that a person might disagree with his decision to go to war in the first place, but who will keep insisting that, as everybody ought to appreciate, it was, after all, *his* decision. What Logue's Agamemnon can't appreciate is that there is a principle at stake. More than that, what he proves incapable of is not asserting himself, and so as the offer of reparation builds through his speech it becomes itself another exhibition of self:

> My summer palace by the Argive sea,
> Its lawns, its curtains in whose depths
> Larks dive above a field of lilies […]
> All this, the greatest benefaction ever known,
> If he agrees to fight. And he admits I am his King.

So much for the tears.

Achilles, of course, as we already know, will have none of it. Our already knowing is Logue's challenge. The battle scenes he can re-invent and make newly fascinating, in part by poetic operations Homer didn't have available to him, by ellipsis and savage juxtaposition; and in part by a casual bloodiness of language that has become one of the hallmarks of the whole project: "His head was opened, egglike, at the back", "Queen Hera whispered: 'Greek cut that bitch.'" It is a different matter to make discursive passages new, to maintain interest where what is at issue is psychological plotting, where the plot and the psychology are so deeply familiar.

Logue's Achilles is beautifully twisted: graceful, courteous, charismatic and bitter. His speech, the speech with which *Cold Calls* concludes, is rhythmically measured, and tonally calm, and betrays all the contradiction of a person eaten up with resentment. "I will not fight for him," he says,

> He aims to personalise my loss.
> Briseis taken from Achilles – standard practice:
> Helen from Menelaos – war.

What really eats at Logue's Achilles is not the loss of Briseis so much as the double standard. The double standard is an effect of personality, an assertion of Agamemnon's right to treat people unequally, and so the merest flicker of that personality is enough to drive Achilles to a double standard of his own:

> Do I hate him? Yes, I hate him. Hate him.
> And should he be afraid of me? He should.
> I want to harm him. I want him to feel pain.
> In his body, and between his ears.

Logue's Achilles is desperately modern, straining to ratchet the argument up to a point of principle, but collapsing back all too quickly into grievance and loathing. The writing is skilful, dramatically shrewd. Character is articulated. Emotional damage is shown to have been done.

Logue's treatment of Homer's book nine comprises the last of the four sections of this instalment of *War Music:* the cold calling – the hollow offers – the title refers to. Prior to that we are on the battlefield, cutting abruptly every so often to the heavens, where the gods display the arbitrariness that is one of Logue's compositional principles. Roughly speaking, as in *All Day Permanent Red*, the earlier sections of *Cold Calls* are culled from books five to eight: Diomed runs amuck, Zeus calls it for the Trojans. But Logue's freedom as an adaptor, rather than a translator, is to smash books up, putting Homer back together in any order he sees fit. The result is significantly and impressively disorientating, almost always we are *in medias res*, voices and agency are constantly shifting. Forms of order do establish themselves – with re-reading a narrative frame comes to assert itself – but the elements of the narrative are kept resolutely alien. We are on a plain. Men are clashing. There is ecstasy in violence. Discussions in the wings are fractured and disingenuous. Power makes itself known by the randomness of its operations. Logue's Homer is kept strange, his war music familiar.

David Herd's *Mandelson! Mandelson! A Memoir* is recently published by Carcanet.

ℬ

Anticyclone Isobars

DOUGLAS HOUSTON

Seán Rafferty, *Poems, Revue Sketches and Fragments*,
Etruscan Books, £9.50, ISBN 1901538311
John Stammers, *Stolen Love Behaviour*,
Picador, £8.99, ISBN 0330433865
Tony Hoagland, *What Narcisscism Means to Me: Selected Poems*,
Bloodaxe Books, £8.95, ISBN 1852246898

After reading his collection, I'm puzzled at Rafferty's neglect by the machinery of literary reputation-making, as his work is often compellingly good. Born in Dumfriesshire in 1909, by the late 1920s he was drawing praise from his contemporary Sorley MacLean for "his brilliance in the Hugh Selwyn Mauberley manner of Pound". In 1932, MacDiarmid called him "the most promising (if not the only) 'modernist' poet amongst us". The poems develop from the Poundian echoes of the 1929 'Return to Wittenberg' sequence to the idiosyncratic modes of later work.

The metrical energy and communicative directness of the border ballad tradition is something of a constant throughout. His verse is already edging towards it behind the Mauberley mask of 'Return to Wittenberg':

> The platitudes of lilac and of rose
> Wearied him, arid the slick
> Competence of sun and moon.
> Horizons tightened round his neck.

The next poem in the book, 'The Red Laird Speaks Out', goes straight into full ballad stride. Its sanguine directness, edge of quirky humour, and simple excellences of rhyme and metre are frequent in much that follows:

> I am the laird of Middleshaw
> although I gang this gait
> a house a byre two fields a copse
> a meadow my estate,
> my two hill fields are stone and whin
> and fire from bush to bush
> a marigold my meadow
> between the tufts of rush.

Some of the work here collected was written for performance and it is in the dialogue pieces that Rafferty's modernist allegiances are often clearest. The Eliot of 'Sweeney Agonistes' lurks behind the disjunctive conversations and syncopated rhythms of 'Maidenhead Revisited' and 'A Serious Thing'. Mordantly effective yet constantly evasive, they valuably extend the range of the book. So too does the richly-imagined free verse account of street acrobats in 'On July 13th', an *homage* to Apollinaire. Elsewhere there is plenty of the offhand satirical swagger typified by 'Said I to my familiar ghost …' and a fullness of halcyon lyricism exemplified in 'Tumbledown Songs'. Rafferty is definitely worth getting to know.

John Stammers's poetry is notable for the success with which he raids the hitherto inarticulate. Much of his work explores the before, during and after of love relationships. Reaching into the silent interstices of self and other, he brings forth remarkably clear and accessible poems, complex in development, sometimes urgent in feeling and always underpinned by an elegant objectivity of tone. With few exceptions, he avoids regular verse forms, the imaginative pressures running through his lines and stanzas modulating the form and music of the work. The poems' success lies in the balance they strike between intense subjectivity and the fullness with which the imagery presents the world. 'Younger', the opening poem, carries the weight of loss that the book conveys recurrently, but Stammers's imagination characteristically defies emotional gravity as he revisits the luminous past:

> I stood in the front of the big studio-window
> and thought I could really see
> the hyper-bright air, the warm days roll in,
> the anticyclone isobars
> drawn languidly across the southern hemisphere of my life.

'Closure' is his hardest-hitting treatment of love's endings, a nine-part sequence of afternoons and mornings through which a marriage falls to pieces. The rawly quotidian detail and plain language that prevail are mediated by the tentative lyricism of a meditation on a photograph of the speaker's parents. "A couple of adulterers", they "grin back at the camera", unknowingly prefiguring their son's predicament. Although man, and woman, hand on misery enough in the collection, it has keenly affirmative and celebratory dimensions. The poems with Italian and American settings are wonderfully responsive to light and provide a strain of exotic opulence. 'La Siesta' demonstrates the power of such imagery in moving from its tragic answer to the question "What is the Earth?" towards the celebratory recognition of life's generosity,

when in clear altering situations
the land exhales the somnolence
of not knowing the source of one's fatigue,
while the blue sky pulses like an hallucination
and fruit follows fruit on the white tables
and great windows, set ajar, cool
in the semi-light [...]

On the lighter side, 'I Don't "Go Organic" Often but When I Do' is an inventive comedy of culinary manners characteristically bright with colourful sensuality of imagery. It ends with "I do not always know what I am doing", indicating the way these poems are so often from the edges of what we know about ourselves yet firmly grounded in common experience.

What Narcisscism Means to Me is Tony Hoagland's first UK collection, bringing together three volumes published in the USA (1990, 1998, 2003). His tone is often discursive, distinctly American, and always deftly directed towards each poem's purposes. He can be disarmingly informal and knows well how to amuse and entertain, but sheer candour and the acuteness of his concerns prevent him from ever seeming casual. Henry Shukman is right on the money in the blurb quote when he speaks of Hoagland's "aggressive moral intelligence". He *boldly goes* all right, confronting topics that include race, gayness and AIDS with an instinct for getting at truth that makes political correctness squirm. The book's title is a self-effacing hook for the intensely subjective impulses behind many of his poems, but, like Stammers, he makes the world vividly apparent, even in metaphorical expositions of selfhood:

How did I come to believe in a government called Tony Hoagland?
with an economy based on flattery and self-protection?
and a sewage system of selective forgetting?
and an extensive history of broken promises?

What did I get in exchange for my little bargain? What did I lose?
Where are my natural resources, my principal imports,
and why is my landscape so full of stony ridges and granite
outcroppings?

The poems cover a wide range, successfully negotiating such major themes as the condition of contemporary America and frequently returning to moving treatments of love and mortality. Many get off to an unspectacular anecdotal start and end up surprising the reader with how much has been mined from incident and reflection. Hoagland is gifted at making accumulations of detail flower suddenly into completed poems and his best effects are large, not conveniently quotable. The voice we hear throughout is invariably clear, engaging, and often slightly acerbic in its avoidances of acceptable half-truths and worse.

Douglas Houston's third collection is *The Welsh Book of the Dead* (Seren, 2000).

ℬ

Going Home

STEVEN MATTHEWS

Derek Walcott, *The Prodigal*,
Faber, £12.99, ISBN 0571226515

If this familiar odyssey of exile and return is what it declares itself to be, Walcott's "last poem", it may arguably leave followers of his career and respecters of his historical significance with an unsatisfied feeling. The problems are partly formal and poetic. But they are also about the presentation of the "prodigal" himself; and, in some senses, they are metaphysical. In the final ten or so pages, this book-length sequence attains a resonant power, leading readers to reflect back on the shaping parable of the work and the use to which it is being put. For most of the time, the prodigal is appropriately astray, lacking in focus and centre. But the fear is that the parable licences tracts of writing here that are themselves cast loose from Walcott's former sources of authority and musicality.

The Prodigal abandons the elaborate experiments with form and rhyme which characterised Walcott's previous collections. The alternately-rhyming lines of *Tiepolo's Hound* (2000) succeeded in holding together the grandeur of the European Renaissance artistic tradition with the more local, impressionistic world of Camille Pissarro – and, by extension, with Walcott's own creativity in various media. The elaborate long lines and rhyme structures of *The Bounty* (1997) opened dangerously towards a world of manifold fruitfulness. This new book adopts a much looser structure, being largely in a blank or free verse reminiscent of some of Walcott's earlier work. Its eighteen major sections, generally divided into four parts, seem to advertise the meandering and episodic nature of this "final" journeying home.

Walcott's has always been a poetry which works by slow accumulations, the intonation of its expansive sentences garnering the multiplicity of what the world holds, both up-close and beyond the horizon. Here, though, the syntactical unfurlings and yearnings can be rhetorically less sure:

> Orange lights
> and brighter in the muffled streets of Zermatt,
> what element more absolute as itself
> than the death-hush of the snow, the voiceless blizzard,
> between the brilliant windows of the stores?

In reaching for the beyond, lineation ("Zermatt / what"), rhythm ("as itself / than"), and grammar ("lights / brighter") often stumble.

Paradoxical attraction towards the "zero" world of mountainous whiteness punctuates the earlier stages of the old man's journey, along with an awareness that such experiences might be duplicitous, "the scene was just like something he had read. / Something in boyhood, before he went abroad." This quandary over the freshness of the exile's experiences is what makes the sequence's first half so unsatisfactory. The scene moves from New York to the Alps to Columbia to Mexico to Milan, Paris, London, to name but a few of the places the wanderer turns up in. Our sympathies are hardly engaged; it is difficult to feel him hard-done by as he appears in yet another alluring situation. In this ironic late reflection upon his career, how seriously are we meant to take the prodigal's assertion that

> approbation had made me an exile [...]
> and then extinction, then the loss of joy,
> but joy in what? In the island or in Italy?
> In the impossibility of, implausibility of,
> Roberta's Venice or Esmeralda's Spain ...?

Whilst it might be possible, in a generous reading, to perceive these as the griefs of a modern Odysseus, relishing every moment of landfall whilst (ha!) keeping his mind set upon home, it is more likely that readers will find the frequent elisions of place and woman plain embarrassing.

> As far as secular angels go there is always one,
> in Venice, in Milan, hardening that horn
> of ageing desire and its devastations [...]

"All these remembered women melt into one"; not since late Yeats has there been such crassly phallic unselfconsciousness on display from a major poet.

Where the blank verse does seem periodically self-aware in the book, it is troubled by the unresolved relation between the experiences narrated and their representativeness. At various moments the central figure is addressed in the third person, and the end of the work tries to assert a firm disjunction between poet and prodigal narrator, whose "home / was the horizon while my own peaks / loomed so inconsolably again". "In my effort to arrive at the third person / has lain the ordeal", declares a directly self-critical voice; and here lies the heart of the curiously overstretched tone of the whole. Earlier poems of the past fifteen years, from 'A Latin Primer' in *The Arkansas Testament* (1987) to 'The Bounty', his elegy for his mother, had seen Walcott in later life emerging as major elegist. Here, news of the death of his twin brother, Roddy, evokes a surprisingly unsustained response, as the speaker continues "listlessly" watching a soccer match on TV.

As a kind of keynote near the beginning, the narrator describes his untimeliness, marooned through his colonial "contradictions" somewhere in the middle of the nineteenth century, and having "missed" the twentieth. Aside from the rhythm, the diction here can seem dated and inert: "aureate Venice", "lissome", "umbrageous", "O to be luminous and exact!", "in what receding year?". For once, at the end of his life, the literary tradition does not seem to help Walcott. In its place is a sadness, almost a desperation, a prodigious self-importance. Only in the final sections, building towards a resurgence of Roddy's spirit as the Lowellian image of a dolphin, does the writing arrive at the kind of orchestration of which the earlier Walcott might be proud:

> they are here.
> Angels and dolphins. The second, first.
> And always certainly, steadily, on the bright rim
> of the world, getting no nearer or nearer, the more
> the bow's wedge shuddered towards it, prodigal,
> that line of light that shines from the other shore.

Steven Matthews's latest book is *Modernism* in the Arnold Context Series, of which he is General Editor.

Under the Sun

PETER FORBES

U. A. Fanthorpe, *Collected Poems 1978–2003*,
Peterloo Poets, £15, ISBN 1904324207

Ursula Fanthorpe is one of British poetry's true originals. Talk of schools and influences is shamed into silence when her name comes up. Her distinctive and productive career after her late start (first book published at fifty) has now been honoured with a *Collected Poems* from Peterloo, her publisher throughout (a Penguin *Selected Poems* excepted).

The really striking thing about Fanthorpe is that in a country in which art has always been distorted by the not-too-hidden injuries of class (for example, Virginia Woolf patronizing and dismissing Arnold Bennett for writing about vulgar industrial life up north instead of the impressions of a life with servants) she writes not from any particular class angle but about humanity.

In truth, she is our Szymborska – making due adjustment for their different political backgrounds. It's not surprising that when the Laureateship was last under contention, Fanthorpe received considerable support, especially from the *Guardian*. If England must have a Laureate she has the right credentials – she has even written, without having to, a poem celebrating Princes Charles on his fiftieth birthday.

It is always wonderful to see a poet celebrated for twenty years whose latest book is her best. It is also extremely rare. A survey of the great and the good in English poetry today would creak with the sound of laurels being rested upon. Not so for Fanthorpe. In *Queueing for the Sun* (2003) her learning and deep sense of history combine with her human sympathy to create really satisfying poems of great power.

There is a lot of history and archaeology in Fanthorpe, beginning with 'Rising Damp', the poem about the "little fervent underground / Rivers of London" that won Third Prize in the first Arvon Poetry Competition (1980) and helped to make her name. In *Queueing for the Sun*, Roman and Celtic Britain are present with vivid force. The explicitly historical poems in this most recent volume are fine but I don't warm to them as much as the poems of common humanity: 'Pottery Class', for instance, which effortlessly slips the idea of the human clay into the stuff that middle-aged people, "Sore from banked-up troubles of a lifetime", slap around for creative relief:

> The sorrowful man sees shapes in his dreams,
> And waking shouts to the night, *I could make that!*

Fanthorpe has always written riddle poems and poems that sound like riddles although they are fully spelt out, and here are some of her finest: 'Waiting Room', 'Needle Work', 'The Vulgar Tongue'. Her commentary on Valentine's Day, 'For Leo on 14.02.2000', has a MacNeicean sprightliness:

> Some whim of the calendar. For who
> Could imagine the birds would woo
> In mid-Feb, when we know quite well
> That it's solstice-onwards that they do?

I am normally resistant to poems about poetry workshops, but 'Workshop's End', about the poignancy of all such short-lived communities, has a universal resonance. Endings feature strongly in Fanthorpe's poetry. 'In Memory' captures perfectly the sense that in life we always fall short and that it sometimes takes a friend's death to recognise what we should have offered in life:

> We are the acquaintances you wanted
> As friends, friends who avoided proper passion,
>
> Lovers who preferred the cordiality
> Of friendship. Your embers reproach us.

The last poem in the book, 'Libraries at War', certainly could be Szymborska (and I mean that as a great compliment). It is a tribute to the power of literature at a time when war was doing its best to destroy a people's resolve and to erase all the fine distinctions of art:

> Fire, fear, dictators all have it in for books.
> The more you destroy them, the louder we call.
>
> When the last book's returned, there is nothing but the dark.

Fanthorpe's vivid sense that history doesn't die but lives on in countless ways, embodied in the present, is encapsulated in 'Driving South'. Where Larkin, travelling in the opposite direction, saw mere surface detail – "An Odeon [...], a cooling tower, / And someone running up to bowl" – Fanthorpe sees:

> The grand, heraldic cruelties, we sense
> Enormous suffering behind each hedge.
> Here a whole village was wiped out, and here
> Hundreds of peasants slowly starved to death.

Fanthorpe's Penguin *Selected Poems* is out of print so this is now the volume to have. I have concentrated on her latest book because it seems to me to mark a new advance in her career. If you like her work already, you'll be buying this book; if you have resisted so far, you really should take another look.

Peter Forbes's *The Gecko's Foot* will be published by Fourth Estate in August.

☙

Paper Music

MICHAEL MURPHY

Peter Porter, *Afterburner*, Picador, £8.99, 0330434365
Dennis O'Driscoll, *New and Selected Poems*, Anvil, £11.95, 0856463736

"I knew I wasn't saying anything like exactly / what I meant, but I knew as well that it was what / I had to say". While I'm not suggesting that Peter Porter had Adorno in mind when writing the title poem of *Afterburner* (neither, I imagine, would he thank me for the comparison, "No paper music, no Adorno rules" being two of the strictures in 'Stravinsky in Hollywood'), nevertheless Porter's search for the least-wrong word maintains a seriousness of purpose analogous to if not coterminus with Adorno's concept of "exact imagination" (*exakte Phantasie*). The meeting and joining of knowledge, experience and aesthetic form in such a way as to foreground art's ability to discover ways of recon-figuring the near-at-hand: to produce work that is both exact, in terms of truth telling, and exacting, in that imagination must rein itself in by remaining true to the world as we know it through the disciplines of science and scholarship.

To discover what might lie on the other side of what it is he said but didn't exactly mean, 'Afterburner' looks to the example of earlier poetic models. Like them, the poem takes its bearings from science:

> Where Jacobean poets used to fill their poems
> with the very latest scientific instances, I reached
> for a handbook a straightaway witnessed 'Afterburn'.
>
> So this was the glow at the tail end of my life [...]

was all the fuel of living left – ahead
the prelinguistic purlieus of the gods.

For a poet as concerned with *civilisé* as is Porter, the idea of slumming it
in an afterlife that returns us to the merely instinctual and which deprives us
of the resources of language is hellish. Equally so is a world governed by
those who trade in the cultivation of fear and loathing: "Donald Rumsfeld's
face is on the box, / Business appointing Murder to the Board". Nor for
Porter the post-ideological aphasia over which Blair had hoped to preside, as
the thirteen epigrams of 'Ideological Moments' spell out.

Seriousness and exactitude, yes; but let's not overlook humour, wit,
tenderness, urbanity and sophistication, the latter being the defining feature
of Porter's steadfast dedication to verse as a craft. For sophistication I read
élan: dash, impetuosity. To be anything other than sophisticated, *Afterburner*
affirms, is to be less than fully human. It is also to give in to mortality, an
unsurprising presence in a collection the book jacket declares to be "late
work". And there *is* something late about this book, as though it were written
in the shadow of Limbo. Hence, perhaps, the dread of being un-committed
(the book ends: "Superior insight – how to stay on the Left for ever") and
boredom. Nothing as grand or *faux* aristocratic as Baudelaire's *spleen* or
ennui – just simple common or garden browned off-edness, the antidote to
which is either a refusal to take gravity too seriously ("Light Verse the right
verse to clothe the truth in") or to put trust in "the God of Repetition (who)
clears / the air of early afternoon of boredom". What repetition affords, of
course, is the promise of continuity; that the present moment won't be the
last, that there'll be many more to come just like it, only different.

Like Porter, Dennis O'Driscoll returns us to the central question of how
we get the world into, as Porter puts it, "impure verse". And it's O'Driscoll's
ability to capture the precious as it co-exists alongside the mundane (Eliot's
"Garlic and sapphires in the mud") that defines the poems gathered here
from six previous collections.

Typically O'Driscoll's poems take the form of, or at least include, lists:
"someone is dressing up for death today, a change of skirt or tie / [...]
someone today is leaving home on business / someone is paring his nails for
the last time, a precious moment"; "A metal clatter of shutters. / A shattering
of the street's silence. / A turning of keys, of unbolting doors. / A reversing of
'CLOSED' verdicts". It's this aspect of his work that has always put me in
mind of the earliest surviving examples we have of writing: baked clay
tablets containing a record of the storage and distribution of grain. The
product of a settled agrarian society, written language came to express a
need similar to Porter's evocation of the God of Repetition: that the future is
if not assured then at least accounted for.

The world seems to have hurt O'Driscoll into verse. There are poems that elegise the familial dead (mother and father, a stillborn baby), and poems which memorably give a voice to those in Ireland who continue to die for political expediency and mistaken allegiances. What marks O'Driscoll's poetry out from, say, Heaney's on this count is a refusal to dress the dead up in the borrowed clothes of myth or the ineluctability of ritual. In 'Mistaken Identity', for example, a prose poem in the form of an interview the like of which O'Driscoll, a civil servant for Irish Customs, must himself have either carried out or overheard, a murdered man speaks of the dailiness of assassination:

> *Can I begin by asking what you were thinking of as the gunman*
> *approached?*

> Nothing very precise, actually. I was vaguely annoyed at pet owners. [...] I'm nearly sure I had a flash of memory also – something reminded me of the nest under the yew at my grandmother's. We found a clutch of warm, fawn eggs one summer there.

Violence, or its threat, is rarely far from O'Driscoll's poems. The stars are "a murder story with the owl's loud screams", while reading a public notice means walking up to it with the wariness of someone "scrutinising a suspect / package, a booby-trapped device". Even when approaching the celebratory, the tone remains circumspect, halting, wary:

> Life gives
> us something
> to live for:
> we will do
> whatever it takes
> to make it last.

O'Driscoll is a recording angel of life's sacred banalities. He does this without censure or snobbery, and without hiding behind a mask of irony. It's difficult to think of another poet who pulls off quite the same trick. *New and Selected Poems* is a significant achievement.

Michael Murphy's *Elsewhere* was published in 2003 by Shoestring Press.

ℬ

Kinds of Pleasure

VICKI BERTRAM

Jackie Kay, *Life Mask*, Bloodaxe, £7.95, ISBN 185224691X
Carole Satyamurti, *Stitching the Dark: New & Selected Poems*,
Bloodaxe, £10.95, ISBN 1852246928
Moniza Alvi, *How the Stone Found Its Voice*,
Bloodaxe, £7.95, ISBN 1852246944

It's hard to say much about three such accomplished and established poets in a thousand words. So, to practise brevity (and in case you're in a hurry), I've selected one word to characterise each poet. The word suggests something about their approach or preoccupations, and something about how it feels to read these collections. Jackie Kay's word is seduction. Moniza Alvi's is distance. And I've chosen consolation for Carole Satyamurti.

If you've got a little longer, I'll explain why. The majority of the poems in Jackie Kay's *Life Mask*, her fourth collection, are concerned with the end of a relationship. Inevitably, it's intimate territory; the book is peopled with "you", "she" and "I". The blurb announces "Kay's most revealing love poems" – a dodgy appeal to the reader as voyeur, but perhaps appropriate: Kay is a performer, adept at transforming her life into art. For the reader, these poems offer the sweet, sad sorrow of (other people's) parting.

Much of the seductive power comes from Kay's ability to make words sing. In 'Spoons' the lovers' sleeping position is turned into a haunting elegy:

> Rusted, the sleeping spoons,
> under the empty moon
> scrap soon, scrap soon
> quine and loon.

This delicious lyricism is tempered by her persona's engagingly forceful personality. The poems draw their power from subtle repetitions and echoes, from cadence and contrast. They are immaculately crafted, poignant, wry and feisty: this is Kay on top form. The use of masks as a unifying theme is inspired, since it complicates an all-too-familiar subject, as well as foregrounding some fine poems about her elusive, theatrical, African father and the experience of sitting as a model for visual artists. Exuberant Maw Broon returns, she too with reason to suspect adultery when her husband's behaviour changes:

> He stapped drinking spilt tea
> Frae his saucer; he didnae belch and say
> Guid fuir me! He didnae tut at the TV.

But like her creator, Maw Broon hymns betrayal like a resilient and charismatic Midas, making it easy to forget just how much it hurts.

Reading Carole Satyamurti's *Stitching the Dark: New and Selected Poems* provides a different kind of pleasure. Her canvas is broad and busy: full of people, chance encounters, journeys, paintings, friends. You feel she is always alert, pen poised, finding subjects in unexpected and unexceptional places: the girl who asks for money to call home, a lizard falling into the rainwater butt. Satyamurti would make a great laureate: prolific, respectful of ordinary people and unafraid to tackle public events like the US soldiers' atrocities at Abu Ghraib in Iraq, or the sinking of the *Herald of Free Enterprise* in 1987. She makes poetry the vehicle for crucial questions about individual and collective responsibility, but she is too warm and involved ever to seem preachy. Formally adept, Satyamurti thinks in and through her poems, rewarding the reader with resonant images, like the peacock's cry described as "broken glass / tearing the heart out of the afternoon", or overblown tulips, "tattered queens with so much death in them".

Death is her greatest theme, and she celebrates the bravery with which people face the discomforts of ageing:

> In old age, when the land begins to tilt, they roll
> like marbles, gently, towards the coast, coming to rest
> in condominiums with impatient gardens, and rules.
>
> [...] They can dance, can swing an iron, and are doing it
>
> for all of us – up ahead, acting impervious
> to tides and weather, to show how one can smile
> beside that slippery remembrancer, the sea.

The "senior" poet of these three, Satyamurti marries thought and emotion in her work. She is prolific but always interesting: quite an achievement in a collection of 225 pages! The longer poems, and the sequences, show her talents best. Although it records so many deaths, *Stitching the Dark* is paradoxically full of life, insight and wisdom.

Moniza Alvi's poetic landscape could not be more different: a vast wilderness dominated by stone and rock, mountains and stars. The title poem is one of a series of brief allegories recording the stalemate of endless global conflict. In one, children are born with guns imprinted in their palms:

Babies had always raged – but
could any child be born knowing,
and prepared for war?

Alvi includes several versions of poems by the French poet Jules Supervielle. Here is one, 'Castaway':

A table quite near to us and a faraway lamp
can't be linked up again in the hostile air.
And right up to the skyline – an empty beach.
A man in the sea is waving, screaming Help!
and his echo replies *What do you mean by that?*

This is poetry at the service of ideas and philosophical inquiry; *How the Stone Found its Voice* expects its readers to work. Alvi is unusual in being utterly uninterested in self-expression or sentiment. Her style is pared and laconic. There are several excellent poems that depict immigrants amidst a blandly uniform English landscape. Plain and economical, they are tremendously evocative:

The luminous Norfolk skies,
the tractors, the gunshots,
the still ponds, the darting rabbits,
cow parsley by the field gates –

all are re-imagining themselves
because Tariq walks in his village,
part of the scene, yet conspicuous,
as if he is walking a tiger.

Alvi is drawn to incongruity, and her distorted, oblique perspectives are grimly humorous. Women waiting for biopsies are depicted as being on a surreal picnic, while a marmalade jar symbolises the process of growing old:

With his stick he pushes coarse amber shreds
To the side, tries to force a path through
The glowing jelly – to my mother, who's faintly
Busy at the base of the jar.

Alvi's poems are like the subject of her 'My Wife' series: elusive, serious, preoccupied and indifferent to audience. Kay offers a seductive dive into the lap and tickle of words dancing. Satyamurti is open to the world around her in all its dazzling variety. Generous and humane, she offers you words as consolation: something, at least, to hold in the face of loss and death.

Vicki Bertram's *Gendering Poetry: Contemporary women and men poets* is recently published by Pandora Press.

ℬ

Time Travellers

JANET PHILLIPS

Carol Rumens, *Collected Poems*, Bloodaxe, £12, ISBN 1852246804
David Constantine, *Collected Poems*, Bloodaxe, £12, ISBN 1852246677

Flowers, statues, clothes, shops, houses, childbirth, relationships: everything is political in Carol Rumens's poetry. The earliest of the fifteen collections represented here challenges the beginnings of unbridled consumerism at the end of the sixties; by the second, Rumens has turned her analytical eye on the Cold War and feminism; more recently residencies in Belfast have given her fertile material; and the last, and new, poem of the book, 'Ordinary Soles', uses a trip to Durham to launch a discussion of the recent anti-war marches. Reading this *Collected* in sequence, you get an impressionistic sense of the movement of European politics in the last third of the twentieth century, as well as an awesome range of form, subject-matter and setting.

Throughout the 'seventies and 'eighties, Rumens tracks the economic shifts taking place in Britain. "We will sell you the lot, we have everything / Our conveyor-strips ceaselessly stride. / This is the exit, here is the sky / carved from a nerveless blaze [...] and the throats of charity tins / cough on cold nickel, your hasty apologies", she writes in 'Superstore'. By 1985 she remembers buying "bright young Grannies / from police states" for her children, whom she "had no right to conceive [...] in such innocence, rosily tumbling / like shabby storks out of the sixties sunset / into the broken-classroomed eighties, beaks / and wings ripped off by the weight of our wire baskets". By 1989, with 'Jarrow', she achieves a supremely controlled anger in this sparsely-rhymed, devastating summing-up of the casualties of Thatcherism:

> Nothing is left to dig, little to make
> A stream of rust where a great ship might grow.
> And where a union-man was hung for show

Nothing is left to dig, little to make.
Night has engulfed both firelit hall and sparrow.

'Jarrow' appears in *From Berlin to Heaven* (1989), which falls half-way through the *Collected*. Here her concerns with East-West European politics dovetail, interestingly, into earlier analyses of the state of marriage. The long title sequence is a tour around a quickly-changing Europe while meditating on the collapse of one relationship and the start of a new one. It picks up connections Rumens has made in its precursor, *Direct Dialling* (1985), between subject and state, wife and husband. "I defect / regularly from those dictatorships / my lovers make of passion," writes the narrator of 'Sixteen Dancers'. The collapse of a political system, the collapse of a marriage: both represent an ideology that has failed to deliver, and Rumens is passionately concerned with the resulting casualties.

The misery of failed marriage is stored up in images of sinister flowers and oppressively cultivated gardens, from the grim estate – "The garden's sand and stones where nothing grows / but a shaggy skull of grass" ('Survival') – to 'Surrey', with "hedges shady as trust funds". These are gloriously subversive. In fact, a reaction against oppression, especially from a feminist standpoint, is often Rumens at her wittiest.

It's as if, in these poems, she has taken her own advice, handed down by an imagined Muse in 'Letters Back': "[…] just try to get the scansion right / And don't come on all tragic. Keep it light". That's not the case, however, with some of the previously uncollected poems included in this volume, which add to the already numerous rakings-over of a failed relationship. But among these uncollected poems I am glad to have had the chance to read 'Metaphysics of the Virgin of Torcello', a carefully patterned, four-stanza riddle about the origins of the sad expression on the face of the renowned statue. The answer is superbly down-to-earth, characteristically showing us the unadorned heart of the matter:

Why she's sad is simply because the stone-setter gave her
Curveless lips and dropped a faint tear from her eyelid
So that all the worshippers, even the weddings and tourists
Are suffused with a gaunt, black limned, soft-golden mosaic sadness
Mixed up by themselves and the artists. And she, wherever she is,
May even be smiling at that.

Statues *per se* don't necessarily populate David Constantine's poetry but his most compelling work is concerned with figures who seem half-way between life and death. Indeed, throughout this *Collected*, the mythic poet Orpheus and the story of his descent into the Underworld and return is a persistent theme. Whereas you get the sense of a life on the move from

Rumens's work, here we find a poet making multiple returns to the same kinds of (Orphic) stories, scenes (portraits of women, undressing; rooms with a sea view), and places (Greece, Cornwall, Wales, and Salford).

Orpheus's lover Eurydice makes an appearance in the first collection represented here, *A Brightness to Cast Shadows* (1980), and she ushers in a series of exquisitely cadenced poems on dying and the afterlife:

> The wind has bared the stars
> The skeletons, the after-images
>
> The life of trees has flown,
> Their swarm of leaves, their hail of birds, their bone-
>
> Dry sticks tap-tap
> Their blades slant in the earth's cold lap.
>
> ('The wind has bared the stars')

Here, too, are the first of some very fine elegies. Two carefully cadenced sonnets on Christ raising Lazurus from the dead are highlights of the second collection, *Watching for Dolphins* (1983). And in *Madder* (1987) we get the entire Orpheus myth in six economic stanzas.

It's not surprising, then, that Constantine was drawn to the story of *Caspar Hauser*, a boy who was incarcerated in darkness with no human contact, from birth until adolescence, and then brought abruptly into the outside world, traumatised and language-less. In Constantine's poem, the characters who look after him take turns narrating the story. Written in spare terza rima over nine cantos, this is an assured narrative, moving with cinematic ease from each character's inner thoughts to the concrete detail of the story's setting. Here is Daumer, a schoolteacher, and the first of Hauser's guardians:

> And Caspar mended, a little, it was never enough,
> For where can you walk in an average town like ours?
> Nowhere, the public squares
>
> Reek, every domicile
> Does its own butchery, a hare hangs
> Bleeding brilliantly at the nostril
>
> From the fist of a woman gossiping in the sun.

Constantine uses a similar rhyme scheme for *Sleeper*, a long account of a train journey, which was previously published as a Delos Press limited edition. *A Poetry Primer*, another limited edition, published in 2004, makes up the penultimate collection.

In the final part of this *Collected* there are new poems which dwell on the ageing process, add to a substantial number of exquisite poems which take flowers as their subject, and celebrate love. In the last, refreshingly playful, poem of the book, the sixty year-old poet takes up a photograph of himself as a baby: "That newborn on the Morrison / Is me […] / Before I had a single English word". But the title of this poem is 'Obolus', the Greek word for the coin used to pay Charon the ferryman for a safe passage to Hades. It's as if his newborn self is already planning a visit to the world of ghosts, a place which this poet continues to sing so poignantly into life.

These two books, by two poets born in the same year, represent two very different writing lives, not least because of gender. Nevertheless, a strength they have in common is a desire to seek out the less visible subjects. "What I have best is often what I lack", writes Rumens in 'Cambridge', and that is what makes the best of the writing here so humane and instructive.

Janet Phillips is editor of *Poetry News*.

℘

Hymns Ancient and Modern

DEBJANI CHATTERJEE

E Powys Mathers, *Black Marigolds & Coloured Stars*,
Anvil, £7.95, ISBN 0856463728
Agha Shahid Ali, *Call Me Ishmael Tonight: A Book of Ghazals*,
W W Norton & Company Ltd, $12.95, ISBN 0393326128
Amir Or, *Poem*, translated by Helena Berg,
Dedalus, £8.99, ISBN 1904556264
Yannis Kondos, *Absurd Athlete*, translated by David Connolly,
Arc Visible Poets, £8.95, ISBN 1900072769

*B*lack Marigolds and *Coloured Stars* were originally published as separate books in 1919, when they introduced twentieth-century Britain to E Powys Mathers (1892-1939), a talented poet who did much to popularise the poetry of the East. This attractive single-volume edition from Anvil should do the same for today's poetry lovers.

Rather than translations, Powys called the former book "an interpretation" of the Sanskrit *Chaurapanchasika* or 'Fifty Stanzas of Chauras' and the latter "versions of fifty Asiatic love poems".

'Black Marigolds' is a poignant love poem. Its narrator is a poet under sentence of death for daring to love a princess. Each stanza is prefaced by the haunting refrain: "Even now". For the poet composing 'Black Marigolds' on his last night, the night is "a black-haired lover on the breasts of day."

The fifty poems in 'Coloured Stars' are versions of a range of poems brought together by the eclectic Powys. They include poems from: "the Japanese of a Courtezan of Nagasaki", "the Arabic of John Duncan", "the Hindustani of Dilsoz (18th Century)", "the Chinese of Ly-Y-Hane", "the Afghan of Muhammadji (19th Century)", "the Persian of Oumara (10th Century)" and "the Burmese of Megdan (19th Century)". These are exotic, often erotic, poems; sometimes with imagery that can seem curious to western readers. In Powys' version of 'Love Song of Thibet' for instance, a lover praises his beloved by comparing her to his goats: her "fine and silky" hair, her "topaz" eyes, her "slight and supple" body and her fresh cheeks all remind him of his flock!

The beauty of the imagery is often striking. In 'Climbing Up to You' Powys writes "Of my heart's blood sweetened to a red grape / For you to bite and swallow and have done." He employs a range of forms, including the two-lined distich, rhyming quatrains, free verse and ghazals (he calls them "gazals"). He deliberately uses some archaisms to convey a sense of the antiquity of these poems, but sometimes his inverted phrases read quite awkwardly.

His "gazals" are lyrical poems about wounded love, but they have no other resemblance to the traditional ghazal. This was, of course, typical of the few ghazals written in or translated into English during the last century.

For anyone interested in the form of the ghazal, *Call Me Ishmael Tonight* is a rare gift. This posthumous collection by Agha Shahid Ali (1949-2001), and the earlier *Ravishing DisUnities: Real Ghazals in English*, which he edited, present the ground rules for what he calls the "American ghazal" and offer ghazals in English that aim to exemplify the formal discipline of this complex form.

A number of ghazals were written for fellow Americans. Many also contain a phrase from other poets whose work Shahid admires: Mirza Ghalib, Ahmad Faraz, Mahmoud Darwish, Gerard Manley Hopkins, and others. The book is thus a wonderful celebration of friendship and of poetry.

Many of these ghazals were written while Shahid was terminally ill, and not unnaturally they sometimes reflect a preoccupation with mortality. There are political couplets too. Shahid was a staunch critic of American policy on Iraq. Ghazals like 'Beyond English' and 'Arabic' show that language is another important issue. In the signature couplet of 'Arabic', Shahid explains the meaning of his name: "Listen: it means 'The Beloved' in Persian, 'witness' in Arabic." But fine as this ghazal is, very many of Shahid's other efforts in this collection are flawed as ghazals. Some don't rhyme, some have lines that are inconsistent in length and metre, while a few have abandoned the crucially important refrain. There are also lines that read most awkwardly, but *Call Me Ishmael Tonight* – the first American solo collection of ghazals in English – is a brave and interesting pioneering effort.

Poem by Amir Or (b. 1956), translated by Helena Berg, does not pretend to be a ghazal, though the entire collection consists of couplets. The language is modern and immediate. The eighteen poems are called "chapters" and have strange titles like the epigrammatic 'The mouth that suckled is the mouth that nurses with a howl'. But the reader who expects a novel or some kind of narrative will be disappointed. Together, the chapters form one long, intense and fluid poem.

Its dramatic opening could be the start of a modern epic. Its Israeli author puts the spotlight on poetry itself: "This poem will be a poem of another century, not different from ours. / This poem will be safely hidden under heaps of words until, // among the last grains in the hourglass, / like a ship in a bottle, it will be seen."

In an *Afterword*, Fiona Sampson says of *Poem*: "In resisting poetic traditions it shows us what poetry can be. It is difficult, paradoxical and beautiful." One difficulty is the constantly shifting perspective: at one moment poetry is being addressed, at another, the reader, or even – as in ghazals – "the beloved". Amir Or ambitiously experiments with writing the ultimate poem, the poem that is like no other; and in the process he creates a protean literary product, modern in outlook but reminding at every step of the very poetic traditions that Or eschews. His content is on the grand scale.

Absurd Athlete by Yannis Kondos (b. 1943) is another collection of poetry in translation, this time from Greek and translated by David Connolly. In 'Computer Memory' Kondos warns that technology has its limitations: "It'll never find / sorrow's square root. Nor / does it care." But poetry can celebrate our humanity. Technology can also be sinister: in 'The House Snake' a telephone is "not / just an oversize snake – from the tales / of olden times –, it's a rattler".

In the title poem modern man is the "absurd athlete" who runs alone "with a headwind" through "fires, wars, grumbling, families" and is "followed by flies, locusts / and civilisation's polluted air." One recalls mythic characters fleeing from the wrath or the amorous passions of Olympian gods. Kondos is a poet who derives strength from tradition to honestly interpret the world he lives in – he is a fine poet of urban angst.

Like Helena Berg, who translated from Or's Hebrew, David Connolly ensures that his translations work as poems in English. As David Constantine's Introduction tells us, this is the test of good translation.

Debjani Chatterjee's recent books include *Namaskar* (Redbeck, 2004) and *Masala* (Macmillan, 2005).

Stand Up and Shout

LUCY ENGLISH

Aisle 16 at the Porter Cellar Bar, Bath, 12 May, 2005
www.aisle16.co.uk

Aisle 16 describe themselves as "a mutant hybrid of the highs and lows of modern culture". They originally met at U.E.A in Norwich, not a likely destination for this brand of urban poetry, but their performance credentials are impressive. Their most recent show, *Powerpoint Version 2.0*, has just had a three week run at the Old Red Lion Theatre in Islington.

First up was Luke Wright. Tall, blond and baby-faced, he led us into an attack on everything modern and ridiculous. Nothing escapes his razor gaze, whether it be Tony Blair, mobile phones or Richard Madeley. "Modern life is tedious and dull, we're on the road, we're on the road, we're on the road to Hull." Simple stuff but the student audience loved it. Next, Ross Sutherland and Chris Hicks took us through a spin of wizard word play and Essex boy humour. Josh Stickley is the weird one. Yes, he does indeed "resemble Jesus of Nazareth", but he knows how to combine ideas for comic effect. 'Snail Racing' and 'Paedophile Prime Minister' were quirky and bizarre and 'The poem that doesn't rhyme' is an inspired piece of ridiculousness.

Loud and irreverent, this foursome stomped their way through the evening.

Aisle 16 are a likeable lot. They banter with the audience and laugh at each others' poems. They have been called "The Boy Band of Poetry": but these are the real hairy, sweaty guys you wake up next to when you have had too many Bacardi Breezers. And this, I think, is their weak side. Yes, they are agile wordsmiths: but listening to them is like listening to next door's student party. They won't turn the sound down.

When they attempted quieter pieces they apologised to the audience. Which was a shame because Chris's poem about pylons in the rain and Ross's lament about his Essex brother were possibly the most interesting poems of the entire evening.

But I don't think the audience of the Cellar Bar shared my concerns. They were young and up for it, like Aisle 16.

Lucy English is a novelist and performance poet, and a lecturer in Creative Writing at Bath Spa University.

ℬ

Bury
Art Gallery
Museum
+Archives

TheText Festival

Opening Times
Tuesday-Friday 10-5
Saturday 10-4.30
& Sunday 1-4

Admission Free
Tel: 0161 253 5878
textfestival.com

19 March -
27 November 2005

Challenging the boundaries
between art and poetry

Exhibitions
Commissions
Performances
Workshops
Publications

Special Events

Introduction to Lawrence Weiner (Talk)
26 July 12.30pm
Bury Art Gallery

Shaun Pickard on Shaun Pickard (Talk)
30 August 12.30pm
Bury Art Gallery

The Poetry of Dom Sylvester (Talk)
27 September 12.30pm
Bury Art Gallery

The Met
Tel: 0161 761 7107

Bury Art Gallery
Tel: 0161 253 5878

Exhibitions

Knitted Poems: Jacqueline Wylie
3 June – 30 July
The Met Arts Centre, Bury

Artists Books
4 June – 31 July
Bury Art Gallery

The Lawrence Weiner Poster Archive
25 June – 4 September
Bury Art Gallery

Radcliffe Riverside Project
2 July – 4 September
Bury Art Gallery

Shaun Pickard
6 August - 16 October
Bury Art Gallery

Different Alphabets
17 September - 27 November
Bury Art Gallery

ENDPAPERS

LETTER FROM IOWA

CHRISTOPHER MERRILL

The auditorium was filled for the memorial tribute to Frank Conroy, director of the Iowa Writers' Workshop and author of the memoir, *Stop-time.* This ceremony *was* a form of stopping time: writers read stories, there was a recording of Frank on the piano (he was an accomplished jazz musician), and at the reception in the Natural History Museum music and drinks were served near panoramas of a prehistoric coral reef and a coal swamp. On a blustery spring afternoon, with rain in the air, my thoughts took a dark turn. April is National Poetry Month in America, and this year we mourned the passing of Robert Creeley, Mona Van Duyn, Thom Gunn, Anthony Hecht, Donald Justice, and Czeslaw Milosz: bold spirits whose works decisively shaped our literary landscape.

Justice was my neighbour, and I had copied a poem of his into my commonplace book not long before he died:

The Small White Churches of the Small White Towns

The twangy, off-key hymns of the poor,
Not musical, but somehow beautiful.
And the paper fans in motion, like little wings.

Iowa City is a small white town of such churches, and if it is more prosperous and progressive than the southern towns of Justice's youth it has its own off-key hymns. He wrote in the cadences of nostalgia, as if he were always preparing himself and his readers for the absences – the title of one of his most important poems – of everything he loved – people and places and the music they made of their lives; the twang he heard informs the best of American poetry, a fractious congregation that seems to unite only in lamenting those who are gone. A remarkable generation of poets is dying off.

The widespread grief occasioned by Creeley's death suggests the centrality of his achievement – a familiar motion in American literature: what was once on the periphery moves to the centre. If I feel closer, temperamentally and aesthetically, to the measured and haunted verses of Hecht, and Van Duyn's intimate explorations of ordinary life, nevertheless I recognize that we are all in Creeley's car: "drive, he sd, for / christ's sake, look / out where yr going" – lines that resonate all the more powerfully now that American foreign policy increasingly resembles a drunken driver.

Gunn and Milosz mapped where we are going with a kind of clarity that brings to mind the witness of Alexis de Tocqueville, still the most reliable guide to the American experiment. The foreign angle of vision, the visitor's dream, the immigrant's inflection – these reinvigorate our poetic discourse. Gunn charts his many changes, Milosz yearns for eternity, and we begin to see our walk in the sun in a different light.

Meanwhile two of the most acclaimed poets from this generation, John Ashbery and W. S. Merwin, show no signs of slowing down. Ashbery's *Where Shall I Wander* is his strongest book in years, while Merwin's *Migration: New & Selected Poems*, a sumptuous gathering of more than a half century's worth of work, suggests that he, too, is not done with his changes. Finally, there is a posthumous love note from A. R. Ammons, *Bosh and Flapdoodle*, which includes several new poems for my commonplace book, among them 'Surface Effects'. Here are some lines to live by:

> Nature, you know, is not a one-way street: its
> most consistent figure is turning – turning
>
> back, turning in, turning around: why?, because
> it has nowhere to go but into itself: all its
>
> motions are intermediate:

All verse is a turning, of course, and the intermediate motions of this generation of poets are coming into focus even as they depart. Theirs was a joyous ride in the dark.

Christopher Merrill's most recent book is *Things of the Hidden God: Journey to the Holy Mountain*. He directs the International Writing Program at the University of Iowa.

ℬ

Julia Darling

Julia Darling, even when very ill, was the most optimistic and uplifting person; grieving for Julia feels like letting her down. She would not have wanted anybody to be miserable, to waste a lovely summer's day.

At least, when a close friend who is a poet dies, the poems are left behind. Each friend can read her poems as if they were specially written for her: each reader can do this because every reader is a kind of a friend. "Friend think of your breath on a cold pane of glass," the lovely 'Indelible Miraculous' begins. The poems in Julia's two wonderful collections of poetry, *Sudden Collapses in Public Places* and *Apology for Absence* (both published by Arc), are generous, clever, witty and moving. They never shrink from a difficult subject matter, death and dying; and yet they have an extraordinary lightness of touch, a humanity and humour, that makes them consoling and comforting. There is a lovely dryness to Julia's humour: "And the past. I could have done without the past." Who except Julia could allow you to face death and look after you at the same time? The poems make you step through pain into another complete world. She makes each a moment of transcendence: each poem contains death and life. They look out at the world then look back in. We get a sense that each person is on her own, with the sea and the natural world, for company. "I would like us to live like two light houses / at the mouth of the river each with her own lamp."

It seems preposterous to even entertain the notion that Julia Darling is dead. Her work continues to inspire and excite people. Her voice is still here. Hundreds of people have written messages and poems to Julia's website since she died. *The Poetry Cure*, which she edited with Cynthia Fuller, is selling like hotcakes. At Newcastle University, where Julia was Fellow in Creative Writing and Health, there are many wonderful and dynamic plans afoot to keep Julia alive.

All of Julia's poetry is life-enhancing, whether it is about death or teenagers, knitting, memory, places, large old men: "Some moments glitter / they land in my arms, / red dawns, wild epiphanies." If it was possible to do something fun, something glorious, Julia would. She was a great one for the spontaneous, for being suddenly extravagant, throwing caution to the wind.

Julia was resourceful, determined, very funny and original. She was creative in every situation, wonderful at bringing disparate and different groups of people together, just as she was talented at getting involved with cross-art projects, the places where poetry meets art and music and drama. Julia Darling was a true original, one out of the box. The ways in which we choose to remember her will hopefully match her, live up to her. She will not be forgotten. She will just get bigger. She will just get better and better.

JACKIE KAY

PR
JUKEBOX

Poetry Review Jukebox is a chance to replay high points from the journal's past. Requests, which should be for material from issues published before 1995, are very welcome – if subject to constraints of space.

Young Soviet Poets
Poetry Review 36:4 (Sept/Oct 1945)

Literary and other activities of young Soviet poets who have recently appeared in print are in one way or another connected with the war [...].

Quite a number of those who showed talent gave their lives for their country. Perhaps the most outstanding of them was Lieutenant Alexei Lebedev, who served with the submarine fleet. His two books of verse published before the war, *Kronstadt* and *Lyrics of the Sea*, contained vivid descriptions of the Baltic seascape. In the first winter of the siege of Leningrad he wrote a great deal and was preparing another book of verse. In the spring of 1942 the submarine he served on was sent on a roving mission in the Baltic. He took with him the manuscript of his new books of poems, most of which he had previously read at writers' meetings, intending to give his verses some finishing touches before sending it to the publishers. The submarine was lost after having sunk several enemy ships, including some warships. All the crew perished. The first two books of Alexei Lebedev's verse have now come out in a new edition.

Semyon Godzenko, who is now 22, took part in the defence of Moscow and Stalingrad, in the Liberation of the Crimea and in the Storming of Belgrade and Vienna. He has been awarded six orders and medals. Before he joined the Red Army as a volunteer he was a student and specialised in Slavonic literature. Since 1942, when some of his verse first appeared in the monthly magazine *Znamya* (*Banner*), he attracted considerable attention. His war poems, which appeared in various periodicals have now been brought out in a small book, *Poems and Ballads,* and have been favourably received by the reading public and critics. The book definitely shows that Godzenko is a forceful and original poet [...].

Soldiers' Song is the title of a small volume of poetry in which are represented ten young poets: Mark Sobol, Oleg Polevoy, Alexander Lissin, Vassili Glotov, Jacob Belinsky, Victor Uran, Vassili Grishayev, Grigory Gorsky, Alexander Romanov and Nikolai Tkachzev. All are officers or men of the Red Army. Their first efforts were published in front line army newspapers [...]. A common feature is the tendency to contrast the creative forces with the destructive properties of the war. The same features are characteristic of Galina Nikolayeva's poems which recently appeared in *Znamya*. She was an army nurse. Her poems are war pictures combined with love motifs. Other young poetesses who have been published are Veronica Tushnova and Galina Morozova, whose poems show excellent technique.

The number of young poets appearing in print is constantly increasing. It is almost a mass invasion of the field of poetry by the young generation [...]. It may perhaps even signify the beginning of a new Soviet poetry.

Nikolai Potashinsky

Thus *Poetry Review*, acknowledging the end of WWII. Semyon Godzenko (died 1953) gained a reputation as a poet of Soviet heroism. *Znamya* (founded 1931, through the Central Committee of the Communist Party) was one of relatively few Russian periodicals to publish through the war. Contributors have included Akhmatova, Pasternak and Pelevin.

LETTERS TO THE EDITOR

dogma 2004: the ten commandments

1. we have no self. the poet does not exist. the words shelley, eliot, plath, duffy are brand names. we offer the collective branding. the cooperative poet. 2. intellectual property is theft. steal (and be stolen from) brazenly. the plagiarist is a coward, hiding behind the myth of the individual artist. we are plagiarists until we learn how to steal. 3. we do not write anecdotes, stories, fictions, histories. our poems are their own space, they exist and edge through language, not through what happened or didn't happen before after or then. 4. we have no family. we have no lovers, they do not need to be prostituted to our reputations. love is an easy generalization for the always-more-complex, always-more-difficult. 5. we do not write poems about other works of art or artists [as] if they are not there in every word we write [...]. 6. we do not write for competitions, we do not write to please our judges [...]if we are offered prizes, we are ashamed, and refuse them. 7. we reject the term 'mainstream' to designate the stagnant poetry establishment, if there is a mainstream it is modernism – a tradition of continuous revolution with the shifting channels of a delta, all contributing. we must refuse to be marginalised, or worse, to make marginalisation a badge of honour. 8. we shun the concepts truth and beauty. we know so much more. 9. "when I see a sentence I hear the sound of feet marching" – norman o. brown. we are at war with the sentence, a guerilla war, and we will terrorize all rhetorics. 10. we do not write to make readers feel. we write to make them think, this means we must think, feeling is merely thought too lazy to think itself. our poetry is the spontaneous overflow of reason.

EDITORIAL

If editorials had titles, this one be would be called "Against Balkanisation". No-one, reading the reviews, citations or recent lectures surrounding it, would pretend contemporary British poetry is just one big happy family. It's unclear, in any case, what such happiness could consist of. Tolstoy was right about the essential predictability of the happy family; or, to put it another way, the boringness of the undifferentiated. But what is it that's not fully achieved when generations mimic each other and siblings wear matching outfits? To extend the metaphor: who, acting like over-protective parents, might be failing to relinquish today's poets, readers or publications into diversity, risk and experiment?

Poetry Review, which, like the Society that publishes it, exists to "help poets and poetry thrive in Britain today", has an obligation to resist poetic monoculture; a monopoly by any single poetic culture. It needs to resist the limits and repetitions inherent in such monoculture, to which difference appears as challenge and in which permitted forms and topics have always already been established. *PR* welcomes the opportunity to publish across groups and generations, against the grain of expectation and personal taste.

"Balkanisation", the term of disparagement for a violent resistance to the resources and splendours of cultural (ethnic, linguistic, religious) diversity, names a turn inward to the repetitions of the identical; and away from the dialogue, appetites and curiosities we deem contemporary. In its return to the familial tribal unit, Balkanisation is superstitious and fearful. The republic of poetry, on the other hand, has always embraced vigour, imagination, creative alternatives. These are among the possibilities poetry may open up across times and conditions. As Neruda says in 'Investigations', "I asked of every thing / if it had / something more, / something more than shape and form / and so I learnt that nothing is empty".

It's unclear what the cut in ACE funding to Peterloo Poets, reported as we go to press, will achieve. Can the loss, one year shy of its thirtieth anniversary, of a press known for its courageous, non-metropolitan independence and high-quality list really contribute to the health and wealth of British poetry? The plan to discontinue Peterloo as a Regularly Funded Organisation would throw the press back onto insecure project funding. While "happy to accept" that Peterloo is a national organisation, ACE would like to see "a correspondingly 'national' programme of development work" further to Peterloo's national competition and submissions policy, regional performances and schools work. Though doubtless this model's ideal for substantial touring companies and venues, it's hard to see what more a one-and-a-half-man press could do. One size fits all?

CONTRIBUTORS

Paul Batchelor is studying for a PhD on Barry MacSweeney's poetry at Newcastle University.

Tara Bergin was born in Dublin and is studying Literature at Newcastle University.

John Burnside's *The Good Neighbour* is recently published by Cape. His latest novel is *Living Nowhere* (Cape, 2003).

Vuyelwa Carlin has published three collections: *Midas' Daughter* (1991), *How We Dream of the Dead* (1995) and *Marble Sky* (2001).

John F. Deane, founder of *Poetry Ireland* and *The Poetry Ireland Review*, is Secretary General of the European Academy of Poetry and a member of Aosdana. *The Instruments of Art* is forthcoming from Carcanet in November.

Ruth Fainlight's latest publications include *Sheba and Solomon*, with Ana Maria Pacheco (Pratt Contemporary Art, 2004), and *Burning Wire* (Bloodaxe, 2002).

Marilyn Hacker is the author of eleven collections of poetry, most recently *Desesperanto* (W.W.Norton, 2003). Her translations from the French include Venus Khoury-Ghata and Claire Malroux.

Tobias Hill has published three collections of poetry, three novels and a book of short stories which won the PEN/Macmillan Silver Pen Award.

Ziba Karbassi was born in Tabriz in 1974 and has lived in exile in London since the late 1980s. She is regarded as one of the best contemporary Iranian poets and has published five collections in Persian.

Jackie Kay's fourth collection, *Life Mask* (Bloodaxe 2005), is a Poetry Book Society Recommendation.

Marzanna Bogumiła Kielar's 1992 debut, *Sacra Conversazione*, won three awards including the Koscielski Foundation Prize (Geneva). She has been translated into sixteen languages: a German collection won the Herman-Lenz-Preis.

Gwyneth Lewis has published six books of poetry in Welsh and English. *Two in a Boat: A Marital Voyage* was published in May by Fourth Estate. She is Wales's first National Poet.

Tim Liardet's *To the God of Rain* (2003) won a Poetry Book Society Recommendation. His fifth collection, *The Blood Choir*, which won an Arts Council England Award, appears from Seren in 2006.

Daljit Nagra's pamphlet *Oh My Rub!* was the first ever PBS Pamphlet Choice, and his poem 'Look We Have Coming To Dover!' won the Forward Prize for Best Individual Poem in 2005.

Sean O'Brien's *Cousin Coat: Selected Poems 1976-2001* appeared in 2002. His version of the *Inferno* is to be published in 2006 by Picador. He is Professor of Poetry at Sheffield Hallam University.

Pascale Petit has recently published *The Huntress* (Seren) and a chapbook, *The Wounded Deer* (Poetry Business).

Maurice Riordan's *Wild Reckoning*, edited with John Burnside, was published by Calouste Gulbenkian Foundation in 2004.

Tomaž Šalamun, a Slovenian poet, will have two new books published in English translation in 2005: *The Book for my Brother* (Harcourt) and *Row* (Arc).

Robert Saxton is the author of two volumes of poetry: *The Promise Clinic* (Enitharmon, 1994) and *Manganese* (Carcanet, 2003).

Henry Shukman's first collection, *In Doctor No's Garden* (Cape 2002), won the Aldeburgh Prize and was a *Guardian* and *Times* Book of the Year. His fiction includes *Darien Dogs* (Cape, 2004) and his first novel, *Sandstorm*, appearing in June.

Pauline Stainer's *The Lady and the Hare: Selected Poems* (Bloodaxe, 2004), now in its second impression, was a Poetry Book Society Choice.

John Stammers's second collection, *Stolen Love Behaviour,* is published by Picador and was Poetry Book Society Choice for Spring 2005.

Matthew Sweeney has just moved to Berlin from Timișoara, Romania. His latest collection, *Sanctuary*, was published by Cape in autumn 2004.

Stephen Watts is a poet, editor, and translator. His most recent books of poetry are *Gramsci & Caruso* (Periplum 2003) and *The Blue Bag* (Aark Arts 2004).

C. K. Williams's most recent book, *The Singing,* won the National Book Award for 2003. His previous book, *Repair*, was awarded the 2000 Pulitzer Prize, and in 2005 he was awarded the Ruth Lilly Poetry Prize.

Jackie Wills's most recent collection is *Fever Tree* (Arc). She was poet in residence at the Aldeburgh Poetry Festival 2004.

Elżbieta Wójcik-Leese translates Polish and British poetry. Publications include *Carnivorous Boy Carnivorous Bird: Poetry from Poland* (co-edited, 2004) and, forthcoming, Kielar *Selected Poems* (Zephyr Press, USA, 2006).